# Doing It For Money

## The Agony and Ecstasy of Writing and Surviving in Hollywood

Edited By

Daryl G. Nickens

for

Published by
Tallfellow® Press, Inc.
1180 S. Beverly Drive
Los Angeles, CA 90035
www.Tallfellow.com
ISBN: 1-931290-58-X
Printed in USA
10 9 8 7 6 5 4 3 2 1

For George Kirgo: *Rara avis nostra volavit...*

# Acknowledgements

If you last long enough in Hollywood, you will have to give a thank-you speech. Every day, someone in Hollywood gets an award. There are professional achievement awards that honor people for what they've done; the innumerable "choice" awards that seem to be as limitless as the number of possible incarnations of choosers. And then there are the myriad private award shows that honor people for just being themselves. Like the self-esteem movement run amok, there seems to be a notion abroad that no child should go home empty-handed.

Sometimes, though, the thank yous are from the heart and to the deserving. So, welcome to the Hollywood Award Show section of this book, where I am honoring everyone who made this book possible.

First and foremost, thank you to the writers whose words of wisdom grace these pages. Without your generosity, it would literally not exist.

It would not exist without my colleagues on the Board of the Writers Guild Foundation, who made possible the most recent *Words into Pictures* Forum of screenwriting, where many of the essays contained here first appeared in the program book.

It wouldn't exist without the patient leadership of Writers Guild Foundation's former Executive Director, Pat Cummings, who understands that organizing writers is like herding cats. And it would not even be the proverbial twinkle in someone's eye without her successor, Angela Wales Kirgo, who wheedled, cajoled, utzed and nagged every contributor to this book, including me. Without Angela, we all would still be staring at blank pages.

This book could not exist without our publishers Leonard Stern and Larry Sloan, the Tallfellows of Tallfellow Press. Your intelligence, insight and old school graciousness is what makes you stand tall. Thank you to them and everyone at Tallfellow: Laura Stern, and especially Claudia Sloan and Bob Lovka, who truly were an editor's editors—most specifically, mine.

Continuing in the award-show vein, your indulgence for two personal thank yous. The first falls under the rubric of the old Hollywood maxim, "Be kind to the little people you meet on the way up because you'll meet them again on the way down." Thank you to special ex-little people, Julia and Matt, my children, who have grown into wonderful young adults, apparently surviving having a father who's a screenwriter. I know the Academy screeners and the occasional movie premier hardly made up for the insanity. Just remember what I've always told you: be thankful—kids in China just have the insanity.

To Salina: for your transforming love and your willingness to be a partner in the insanity, mere words cannot express the depth of my gratitude. But since I'm donating my royalties from editing this book to the Writers Guild Foundation, mere words will have to do.

And last of all to you, the reader, go my thanks and the hope that you have found this to be the kind of book I wish had been available when I was starting out: one that teaches, inspires and reveals; but most of all, becomes a trusted friend to be sought out whenever you have need of the truth.

To paraphrase one of the greatest thank-you speeches in Hollywood history: I hope you like it, you really like it...

Daryl G. Nickens
Editor

# Table of Contents

*"There's nothing to writing. All you do is sit down at a typewriter and open a vein."*

—Red Smith

# Preface

Molière once said writing is like prostitution: first you do it for love, then for a few close friends, and then for money.

The irony, of course, is that Molière knew it's always been a lot easier to sell your charms than your words.

Today, selling your words to screen and television—doing it for money in Hollywood—is a real-life mission improbable. Doing it for a living is a miracle.

Yet, everyday a ragtag band of miracle workers does just that. They write the stories told and retold around the global campfire that is today's film and television industry. Their words are their livelihood–and the industry's lifeblood.

Who are these undaunted souls? They are professional screen and television writers. The men and women who're doing it for money in Hollywood.

These are their stories.

Tales of toil and triumph. The blank page. The struggle to create. The journey through the darkness of development hell to the light of movie and television screens around the planet. The agony and ecstasy of doing it for money.

To bring order to this journey through the chaos of the creative process, I've organized each chapter by theme: from the writing process itself (aka, writing avoidance); to breaking into the business; to pitching and selling; to the production process; to collaboration (aka, writer avoidance); and, finally, to those moments of personal triumph and revelation that, in the end, are why it's not really about the money.

If you are one of those wretched souls who, rather than be scared off by these dispatches from the belly of the beast, is inspired to exclaim, "Ah, this is for me!," there is something special in these pages for you. I have included "Secrets of the Hollywood Pros" at the end of each chapter: practical, "how-to" advice from top writers. Want to know how you get an agent? Avoid getting nailed by the Script Police? Take notes without taking hostages? The writers who share their hard-won knowledge of how it works in Hollywood will tell you how to do all that—and more.

If this is starting to sound like a late-night Ginzu knife commercial, that is only because my hope for this book is that it becomes your Swiss Army knife of screenwriting books—the one that's always with you not merely because it's clever, but because it's useful: whatever the problem, it's got what you need.

And if you need to know about doing it for money in Hollywood, then this is where to read all about it.

Editor

# THE AGONY

*"I love being a writer. What I can't stand is the paperwork."*

—Peter De Vries

# Chapter 1

## INTRODUCTION

## I Only Take Phone Calls When I'm Writing:

## The Writing Process

---

Who really likes writing? Not most professional writers.

Admitttedly, writing seems to beat real work. In fact, using the word "work" to describe a day spent nursing a latte at Starbucks while staring at a laptop screen doing "research" on the Internet might even seem terminally narcissistic. But that's because the real work of writing is, like magic, in what you don't see. The screenwriter is a conjurer who creates a castle in the air that somebody with real money wants to move into. Doing this successfully is real work. If only screen and TV writers could rip open their skulls and show their psyches, the carnage and scar tissue would put a stevedore's mitts to shame. "Ya see this here? Got it pitchin' a feature at Disney." Or, "Check out this baby. Series on NB-fuckin'-C." Or, "Ain't that a beaut? Two words. Meg Ryan." Suffice it to say, there're reasons why Samuel Johnson said, "No man but a Blockhead ever wrote except for money."

---

Not that doing it for money makes the process of writing any easier. Writing for money is like marrying for money: you earn every penny. I have calculated that no matter how much money I'm paid for a script, when that amount is divided by the time I actually spent writing, added to the amount of time I spent worrying about what I was going to write, multiplied by that constant, innervating dissatisfaction with whatever I've written thus far—all of which increase in direct proportion to the amount of money I'm paid—my hourly wage always comes out to about the same as being paid to say, "Can I supersize that for ya?"

Working for yourself is no better. When you write a spec script—whether to sell, to break in or to reinvent yourself—the rush of creative exhilaration born of promulgating your brilliant vision your way invariably gives way to the realization that you're working for someone who is impossible to please and unable to pay.

So if writing sucks big time, why do it?

Remember the ending Marshall Brickman and Woody Allen wrote for *Annie Hall*?

> ALLY (V.O.)
> This guy goes to a psychiatrist
> and says, "Doc, uh, my brother's crazy.
> He thinks he's a chicken." And, uh,
> the doctor says, "Well, why don't
> you turn him in?" And the guy says,
> "I would, but I need the eggs."

The answer is simple: writers are nuts. And, as the essays in Chapter One reveal, we need the ecstasy of creation so much that we will endure the agony of laying our own eggs.

# Phil Alden Robinson

## How I Write

---

*"Now, finally, there are no more distractions, all the possible procrastinations are gone, you're primed and inspired to start writing."*

Phil Alden Robinson wrote (or co-wrote) *All of Me, In the Mood, Field of Dreams, Sneakers* and *Freedom Song,* but wishes he'd written *Chinatown.*

This is my writing routine. I follow it religiously, and I *highly recommend* it.

I do not get up early on the days I write as I don't want to be groggy. In fact, to prevent grogginess, I sleep as late as possible, then feed the dog, exercise (very good for clearing the head before writing), take a long shower (good thinking can be done here), eat a healthy breakfast (very important to prepare you for writing), read the newspapers (sharpens your mind), make some phone calls and do all the assorted little things around the house that have piled up to get them out of the way so they don't give you an excuse later for not writing.

Now it's time for lunch. I make it a point to go out to eat, having found that getting out of the house is an excellent way to clear the mind for writing. Lunch invariably leads to an errand or two, maybe a little shopping, sometimes even involving the purchase of items without which one cannot write, such as paper, a nice pencil, or a book that you may someday need for research.

When you get home, there's mail to answer and phone calls to

---

return, all of which are very important to get out of the way so they don't interrupt your writing later. By late afternoon, you're faced with a dilemma: start writing now, only to have to interrupt it for dinner, thus losing valuable momentum and focus… or put it off until after dinner. I highly recommend you *not* start writing at this point. Most people are not at their peak in the late afternoons, and there's nothing worse than getting a head of steam going only to cut it off prematurely. So now's a good time for catching up on magazines, one of which might actually contain a nugget that inspires or informs your work.

After dinner, you realize there's a movie you've been putting off seeing, and let's be honest here: how can we be so presumptuous as to write movies if we're not seeing them? It is absolutely crucial that we learn from our peers, profit from their mistakes, and experience first-hand what the audience likes and dislikes.

Okay. The movie lets out at ten and home you go. Now, finally, there are no more distractions, all the possible procrastinations are gone, you're primed and inspired to start writing.

But here's the thing. If you start writing now, you'll be up until 2 or 3 in the morning, and that's going to screw up tomorrow something fierce, so I urge you to go right to bed. The next morning, be sure not to get up too early, as you don't want to be groggy on a day when you're writing… and repeat all the above steps.

I do this for weeks—sometimes months—on end until I feel so guilty and fraudulent that I drop *everything*, turn off the phones, and do nothing but write from morning till night until I'm done.

# Stephen Gaghan

## Fade the Fuck in:

---

*"Finally, I get down on my knees and beg God to allow me to write the worst sentence ever written..."*

Stephen Gaghan won the Emmy® for Best Dramatic Writing in 1997 for an episode of *NYPD Blue* and the Academy Award® for Best Adapted Screenplay in 2001 for *Traffic*. He wrote the screenplay for and directed his most recent film, *Syriana*.

This is the dread time, the in-between time, dead time, my time, time. A time-I-loathe time. A word I loathe, time. An ugly, clipped word, insignificant and unfinished. Stare at it for longer than an instant and it begins to look like an herb or a piece of thread brushed off a sweater in a waiting room. Anything and nothing. Time. Time. Time. It's seven-thirty in the morning and I haven't started; eight-oh-five and I haven't started; it's nine-thirty, what is wrong with me? Where's the timer? I'll set it to five minutes and when it rings I'll be started, no matter what. I'll set it to one minute and that's it, one minute and no matter what, I'll be started.

Obviously, the problem is the idea, the job, the pay, the people, the underlying material, the lack of underlying material, too much research, not enough research. Obviously, the problem is me. I am the problem. I am a fraud. The problem is, I am a fraudulent human being who has lucked out completely up to now and now the luck has completely run out. The problem is, I am a phony with no ideas and logorrhea, that is the problem that got me into this. I am a phony who talks the talk without walking the walk, constructed of smoke without any fire, wearing a large hat, but owning no ranch: a blabbing homeless smoke figure with a large head made of hat.

Obviously, I should never have signed on for this, but I can get out of it. I can quit. I'll call them up and explain. I'll explain I've had a change of heart, a seizure of confidence, I've grown confused from all the reading, I'll recommend other people, I'll bow out gracefully. If it was my idea, it's a bad idea; if it was their idea, then I never understood it; if it was my idea that I've told no one about, then this hasn't even happened. It's almost ten. It's ten o'clock in the morning. This day is shot.

Obviously, I have other things to do. There are myriad important things that have been left hanging, just hanging around, loose ends, errands. Errands are good. I'll just hurry out in a huff, a self-important huff, with the air of a man hurrying on his way to do important things that must get done. No, impossible, I refuse. I refuse to be that person, that person on the sidewalk in a daze clutching his little list of important errands, talking on the telephone while trying on new shoes.

Obviously, the problem is my desk. My desk is such a mess if only you could see my desk: there are piles stacked sideways on top of piles, unread biographies written by people whose other biographies I have loved, biographies of people who have specialized in the writing of biographies; there are gifts to be delivered, pictures of children, books to be adapted, books to be returned, information on voting in primary elections, notebooks, legal pads, mounds of legal pads filled with notes, tiny scraps of paper scribbled with dialogue; a variety of devices used for the

writing of notes while walking around, driving, doing anything
other than what I should be doing. Yes, the problem is the desk.
When the desk is orderly, I will begin. It is a present to me from
me about me. A neat desk is a gift to me. The books go on shelves.
The notebooks are stacked. The little grubby scraps of brilliant
dialogue go in a shoebox and that shoebox can be lost somewhere
in the future between moves like all the rest.

You should see this desk. It's beautiful. The grain of the wood
is beautiful. The pens in the silver julep cup are beautiful. The
stapler and pencil sharpener and translucent tape are in a perfect
little north-south row. The laptop sits on its ergonomically correct
platform. The chair with breathable mesh and lumbar support and
technology used in spacecraft is exactly the right height. My
elbows are at my sides, my wrists extended in delicate, anti-carpal
harmony. The light off the water through the windows is cheerful
but not too bright, playing on the ceiling. I breathe deeply and
stare, stare, stare at the blank screen, the flashing cursor. Finally, I
get down on my knees and beg God to allow me to write the worst
sentence ever written: Please God help me write one lousy
sentence, the worst sentence ever written by man, please.

# Dan Petrie, Jr.

## The Agony and the Ecstasy of Daniel Petrie, Jr.

---

*"I'll call Peter, he's got a good shrink, and he hates writing as much as I do."*

Dan Petrie, Jr. wrote and directed the TNT original movie *Framed* starring Rob Lowe and Sam Neill. He also wrote the films *Beverly Hills Cop* and *The Big Easy* and co-wrote and directed *Toy Soldiers*. Petrie has served three terms as President of the Writers Guild of America, west.

PART ONE: THE AGONY

FADE IN:

INT. HOSPITAL — DAY

Great. This script sucks already. Who opens a movie with an interior?

EXT. HOSPITAL — DAY

Could that be any more generic? What's a good name for a Cincinnati hospital? Thank God for Google. "You've got mail"— duh, of course I have mail. When do I not have mail? It's all junk, though. No, wait, it's not. Ashcroft did what? Oh, my God, it's true: he's singing. I hate forwarding stuff, but that's just too funny. What did I sign on for? Oh, right, Google, hospitals, Cincinnati.

EXT. MOUNT ST. MARY'S HOSPITAL — DAY

Or does that automatically make the cop a Catholic? Why not, though? Who cares? Let's just get on with it. Jesus. Okay:

An ambulance screams up to the emergency entrance of this mid-size Cincinnati hospital.

This is bullshit, there's nobody we know in that ambulance, this is just a lame way of disguising what's basically an establishing shot, and is there anything more boring than an establishing shot? Well, yes—sitting here trying to write this stupid thing is more boring. I could be directing right now—why the hell did I pass on two perfectly good pictures? What was I thinking? Yeah, yeah, I know, they sucked. But they didn't suck as much as this one does. I should have my head examined. You know, that's not a bad idea: I should have my head examined. Why do I always make this so hard? You'd think this was my first script. Actually my first script was a lot easier. Why can't I just start the damn thing? I'll call Peter, he's got a good shrink, and he hates writing as much as I do. What's the name of that new pill? Elixon? Effexin? Efferdent? I really am going crazy. I don't need to take a pill to help me start writing, for God's sake. Oh, bullshit—of course I need a pill. I sure need something. If not a pill, what? Electroshock? The question is, could a pill really help? I wish I knew how to spell the name of that new pill. Wait—I should just be able to enter "writing" and "antidepressant" in Google....

...that was depressing. What? "You have spent 136 minutes online. Your pricing plan for this billing cycle is for unlimited use." Great. Time is money. At least I'm saving money while I'm wasting time. That could be their slogan: "AOL—where procrastination gets a volume discount." But this is a record, even for me. It's 4:30 and look what I've got:

EXT. MOUNT ST. MARY'S HOSPITAL – DAY

That's progress, considering I've only been sitting in this chair for the past seven fucking hours. And for what? An establishing shot? Who says you can't open with an interior? Let's just start the damn story.

INT. MOUNT ST. MARY'S HOSPITAL – DAY

Okay, not a bad opening—if this was *Touched by an Angel*. Anyway, why does this hospital need to have a name? It's not like we're coming back to this location. It'll read better if it has a name. Wait a second. Hold on. Read better? This is a rough first draft. Nobody's going to read my rough first draft. Since when have I not rewritten a rough first draft before it goes out? If it really needs a name for the read, I can add it then. I'm just totally distracting myself by even thinking about this now.

FADE IN:


INT. HOSPITAL—DAY


Nice. Full circle—and in less than a day, too. And that's a day I'll never get back. God, if I could at least get a page done before dinner, I wouldn't have to go through this tomorrow. Yes, I would. But not as bad. Okay, almost as bad. Not quite. Bad minus one percent. Dinner's at 8:00? Plenty of time to write a page, what's it now, 5:00? Wow, 5:30. The restaurant's on that side of the hill, so we should leave at 7:30. That's still two hours, plenty of time. But I'm always doing this, starting something at the eleventh hour, then I wind up running around, trying to get ready at the last minute, which makes us fifteen minutes late for everything, and Connie hates that. But if I get in the shower now...


PART TWO: THE ECSTASY


FADE OUT.

# SECRETS OF THE HOLLYWOOD PROS #1:

## Getting Into The Flow

Linda Ringer, Ph. D., a psychologist specializing in creative artists, works with writers on the process of writing. In addition to consulting with individual writers, Linda gives classes on the creative process at UCLA Extension, the Esalen Institute and the American Film Institute. But just because she treats writer's block is no guarantee she doesn't get it, too. Here's how the good doctor cures herself:

What do I do when I am not "in the flow?"

In my worst blocked moments, I make one cup of coffee after another, pace about the house, and indulge in ruminating, brooding, obsessive behavior, erroneously believing the pain will dredge something up in me. I usually end up with a caffeine-induced stomachache, which conveniently gives me the excuse to rent a movie and attempt writing tomorrow. If I am in a somewhat better head space, I reach for my vitamins... heat up some green tea... and clean out my closets. Moving up the continuum from unhealthy to healthy "blocked" behavior, I will engage in activities which inspire me: take a brisk walk and smell the eucalyptus trees, light a candle and listen to Spanish monks chanting, dance to Van Morrison and visit the art gallery down the street. In my healthiest blocked—or shall we say "challenged" times—I do as I teach! Bring out my journal, ask myself what the anxiety is really about and stream-of-consciousness write about whatever comes up for me. Then, I will dialogue back and forth between my anxiety and my wise inner self. Tapping a loving place within, I am able to give myself the encouragement and faith I need to write the pages for today.

I am "in the flow."

*"In Hollywood the woods are full of people that learned to write but evidently can't read. If they could read their stuff, they'd stop writing."*

—Will Rogers

# Chapter 2

## INTRODUCTION

## Breaking and Entering:

## How Miracles Sometimes Happen

Hollywood is a tough town.

How tough? Let me quantify it for you.

The most recent Annual Report of the Writers Guild of America, west lists total membership as: 7,723 Current members; 336 Associate members (defined as writers who have worked once under Guild jurisdiction, but didn't earn enough credit to become Current members); and 1,127 Post Current members (writers who have been current members for at least ten years, but have lapsed from Current status because of lack of employment under Guild jurisdiction). That's a grand total of 9,186 people. Except for a few writers who've written independent films but never worked for a Hollywood company under WGA jurisdiction, a similarly small number of animation writers who've never worked in live action or on WGA-covered animation such as *The Simpsons*, and the few members of the Writers Guild East who are not also members of the Writers Guild, west (mostly, but not exclusively, news writers and soap opera writers), these 9,186 souls are essentially the universe of writers currently alive who have ever worked professionally in Hollywood as writers for movies or television.

Discouraged? Wait, there's more.

The Guild reports an employment rate of 53.7%, which means that at any one time, only 4,933 of these 9,186 writers are working. The same report indicated that there were only 5,064 individual employments among Guild members.

Depressed? Keep reading.

If you use those 5,064 individual employments as a rough approximation of the order of magnitude of the number of writing jobs in Hollywood, and factor in that you, who just arrived in town with 120 pages of the "Best Goddamn Screenplay You Ever Read" in your arms, will be competing for one of those absurdly limited opportunities against the 9,186 writers in the Guild plus the thousands of professional actors, directors, editors, cinematographers, grips, production designers, sound engineers and producers, managers, agents, assistants, etc., etc. already working in the business who not only have the "Best Goddamn Screenplay You Ever Read" under their arms, but actually know "Somebody Very Important" in the business to give it to… and then factor in all the former agents, former executives, former assistants, former spouses of the formerly powerful, not to mention the waiters, waitresses, hairdressers, taxi drivers, valets, chauffeurs, video store clerks, diet consultants, spiritual advisors, yoga instructors, martial arts instructors, masseuses, steam-bath attendants, doctors, lawyers, dentists, accountants, stockbrokers, financial advisors, real estate agents, dog groomers and dog walkers to the STARS, and, of course, everybody else in Hollywood who's just finished writing the "Best Goddamn Screenplay You Ever Read" and has a connection to "Somebody Really Important (Whom I'm Not At Liberty To Discuss)"… then take into account the thousands of graduates of the world's elite film schools who come to Hollywood each year because they've not only written the "Best Goddamn Screenplay You Ever Read," but directed the "Best Goddamn Student Film Ever Made" (which took top prize at the "Most Prestigious Goddamn Film Festival On The Planet")… it all adds up to this:

Go back to Iowa.

—THE END—

Okay, now that we've scared off everyone whose heart isn't really in it, here's the good news:

Every day somebody makes it.

Remember those 336 Associate members of the Guild? Somehow—by hook or by crook—they made it. In fact, the one thing that absolutely everyone who's in the Writers Guild has in common is that at one time, they weren't in it. Each of us was once on the outside trying to make a miracle happen.

It happened for us. It can happen for you.

But it doesn't just happen. Every story of a writer's good luck in Hollywood contains a version of Louis Pasteur's observation that luck favors the prepared. In Hollywood, luck also favors the indomitable. Writer and script consultant Dennis Foley may have said it best when he noted that, "Hollywood is the only town where you cannot fail. You can only quit trying."

So, the bottom line is: anytime you want to see that miracle worker who's going to jump-start your career, just look in the mirror.

And, as you will see in the following essays, that may be the best news of all....

# Bob Cochran

## Breaking In: A Primer

---

*"He said: 'I'm sitting here trying to find one word in this script that I like, and I can't.'"*

Bob Cochran has written and/or produced a number of shows, including L.A. Law, The Commish, JAG and La Femme Nikita. Most recently, he co-created 24 and co-wrote the pilot episode, for which he co-received an Emmy®.

Breaking into television as a writer really isn't all that difficult. I knew this because when I was first starting out, I met David E. Kelley and heard how he did it. He'd been a lawyer in Boston, written a spec feature about lawyers which got sold and produced, then moved out to L.A., where he met Steven Bochco and got on staff at *L.A. Law* and became famous and successful.

I was a lawyer, too, and had also written a spec feature about lawyers. I already lived in L.A., so I was a leg up on David Kelley right there. A friend got my script to Steven Bochco who liked it well enough to bring me in to pitch (that's how I met David Kelley). They gave me an assignment and I immediately quit my job. Why not? That's what David Kelley did, and apart from my feature not getting sold, I was right on track with him.

I wrote the script and turned it in and was thanked politely for my work which was completely rewritten and virtually unrecognizable when I saw it on screen. But I wasn't too discouraged. I had an assignment under my belt and, apart from not selling a feature and not getting hired on staff, I was still right on track.

Then the writer's strike hit and I was out of work for five months. My savings dwindled rapidly and I fell into debt and meanwhile my wife gave birth to our first child. The strike ended and eventually I got another assignment. This time, I felt like I knew what I was doing and was confident things would work out. I was thanked politely for my work which was completely rewritten and virtually unrecognizable when I saw it on screen. Nevertheless, apart from not selling a feature and being out of work for five months and being nearly broke with a newborn child and having failed, twice, to be hired on the staff of a show, I was still more or less on track.

I managed to get a third assignment, this one from an executive producer, call him Phil, who claimed he liked working with new writers. I turned in the script, secure in the knowledge that I could only be getting better with experience. After a couple of days, Phil called. He said: "I'm sitting here trying to find one word in this script that I like, and I can't." Then he hung up.

Apart from not selling a feature, being short on funds, having failed three times...

I called my old boss and everyone else I knew and began looking for a real job. (Meanwhile, I met with Phil, who spent five grueling hours dragging me through every word of my script, explaining why it was bad and, sometimes, how it could be made better. In retrospect, it was the best thing that ever happened to me as a writer, but at the time I felt like Mike Tyson's sparring partner. I just wanted to get out of The Business in one piece.)

Then my agent called and convinced me to take one more

meeting, with a prime-time soap which was in its last year. The producers were new to the show and looking for someone with a legal and financial background to help with the wheeler-dealer aspects of the series. I met with them, talked law and business for a while, then left.

That night, my agent called and said they wanted to hire me on staff. I said, Just like that, I don't even have to write a script? He said, Right, they just want someone to help them come up with law and business angles to hang stories on. Next day, I had an office of my own.

So there you have it. I can't speak for David Kelley, but for me the trick was simple: I had to get hired before the people that hired me actually read anything I'd written. All of which only confirmed what I'd thought from the start. Breaking into television as a writer really isn't all that difficult.

# Steven Rogers

## Easy Writer

---

*"Write what's important to you."*

Steven Rogers wrote or worked on *Hope Floats*, *Stepmom*, *Kate & Leopold*, *Ever After* and *Earthly Possessions* and is in preproduction on *P.S. I Love You* and *Flora Plum*. He is extraordinarily good-looking for a writer.

People sometimes ask me, how can they make it as a writer. Truthfully, you have to sleep with a lot of people... A LOT. And here are the names:

No, the truth is, I really have no idea, but this is what happened to me.

I had never written a screenplay before. I never went to college. I had no industry connections or thoughts of becoming a writer. I came to Los Angeles as an actor touring in a play. I won a prize for it, so I immediately moved out here. I figured, no one in New York was giving me a prize, so what was I doing there? It was only after I'd been here a few months that I found out EVERYONE who does a play in Los Angeles gets a prize, but by then it was too late. Once here, I wanted to be in movies but movies didn't want me. So while I was delivering pizzas for Maria's Italian Kitchen (Maria is neither Italian nor a woman, by the way), I started writing a screenplay just so I could act in it. I didn't think about being commercial or about structure. Only about what I had to say. I wrote the script in three weeks because I didn't know that was fast.

Around this time, I was invited to go to Europe. I had less than no money, so I threw a big party for myself. I invited all my friends and made them give me ten bucks each. It worked. I have a lot of friends. In fact, I have friends I haven't even used yet. I made gobs of cash and left town. But before I went, I gave my script to a friend who was working at the Travel Lodge in Culver City. Did I mention I had no connections? She and I had each been writing scripts and reading bits back to each other, telling the other how remarkable our work was. Important to do. I figured she'd give me notes. Instead, she passed it around, encouraging people to read it.

When I returned, it had been passed to Elizabeth Seldes, an executive at MGM. God bless Elizabeth Seldes. She asked if I had a literary agent. I barely had a legit agent, but why tell her that? I said no and she said she'd give it to a couple of agents and if they liked it, they would call. The following week: CAA, ICM, WILLIAM MORRIS, UTA all called. And they weren't saying come in and pitch yourself to us. They were saying come in and let us pitch our agency to you. I stopped answering my phone just so I could play their messages for my friends. I couldn't wrap my head around it.

I made appointments to meet all the agents alphabetically and on the same day. A mistake. And probably too nerdy to admit to. One agent told me all the other agencies just wanted me for this one script and then would drop me like a hot tomato (I think he meant potato). Another asked what was happening with the script? When I told him Elizabeth Seldes liked it and MGM was reading it over the weekend, he told me without hesitation that I blew it.

Big time! He said if MGM passed, everyone in town would know it and I'd be dead in the water. I tried to figure out how he got that scenario from my telling him Elizabeth Seldes LIKED it?!

By the time I got to UTA (the last on the list alphabetically), I was pretty much out of the box. When the agent asked what the status of the script was, I told him I blew it. I gave it to that awful Elizabeth Seldes and if MGM passed I'd be dead in the water.

He basically told me to shut up.

He said there were probably 25 places to go with this script. If MGM passed there'd be 24.

Needless to say, I picked him.

I got lucky. I might not know the one true way to make it as a writer, but this is what I do know: What happened to me can happen to anyone and it does. Have confidence and get lucky. If you don't have confidence, get it. If you can't get it, fake it. Don't let other people discourage you. People will say anything and they're mostly wrong. Don't write something just to be commercial. Write what's important to you. 'Cause that's how you find your own voice and that voice will be what people respond to. Surround yourself with friends who support you and share your ideals and your standards. Fight with them and fight for them and support each other. Be unique. Use your spirit. Use your vision. And aspire to something great.

The script sold for gobs of money, by the way.

# Naomi Foner Gyllenhaal

## Where I Learned To Write

*"It's about what needs to get out there."*

Naomi Foner Gyllenhaal was involved with the development of *Sesame Street* and *The Electric Company* at the Children's Television workshop. She received an Academy Award® nomination, a Golden Globe and a PEN West Award for her screenplay *Running on Empty*. Her other credits include *Losing Isaiah* and the adaptation of *Bee Season*. Her children, Maggie and Jake, are actors. She's still waiting for the ultimate accolade: a blue ribbon for one of her cucumbers from the Martha's Vineyard Agricultural Fair.

I learned to write on *Sesame Street*. Really. Big Bird and Oscar® taught me the basics. You had to know who you wanted to reach with a particular set of ideas. Then you had to figure out how best to accomplish it. It seemed simple. It wasn't.

Not every audience was seduced the same way. Some, like the four year olds we were attempting to teach the alphabet, didn't sit still very long. And they didn't control the remote. So we had to reach their parents as well to get to them. We peppered the show with celebs we thought would keep the parents' attention and added jokes that went right over the heads of the four year olds to amuse the moms and dads. When we could, we tried to make them all laugh.

We had already noticed that big advertising companies had managed to get generations of preliterate kids to pester their parents' to pull a particular cereal from the supermarket shelf. We used the same tactics to a more altruistic end. We employed teams of researchers and academics to tell us about the kids we were trying to reach and a variety of creative people to use the information to accomplish it. We learned to talk across the table to each other and eventually to them. We changed the culture.

I took the lessons I learned on Sesame Street with me to Hollywood. It seemed obvious. By then, I had an agenda. Politics. I wanted to change things. We had already started with *Sesame Street*. Black faces were appearing regularly on television where they had never appeared before. And the unspoken message was it was okay to be Black. Unspoken messages were very powerful. Ethnic children who a few years before were choosing white dolls in self-esteem testing were now picking dolls that looked like them.

I thought we could do the same for grown-ups. Model ideas that were out of the mainstream. Reach a specific audience with particular information. A big audience. Tell the stories that were going untold.

I developed what I thought of as "the trickle-up theory." If you moved people with the story of a particular character, they might think about the bigger issues implied in the smaller story when they stopped crying or laughing or laughing through their tears. *The Diary of Anne Frank* had moved more of us than all the statistics about the Holocaust. Archie Bunker had changed more people's minds than any Sunday sermon. The power of the specific. It works. An agenda. An audience. An intention. Something happening to someone just like you.

What I didn't count on was that there were people who didn't want the stories told. Some of them didn't even know it. But they fought like the dickens.

Look where we are today. Women over forty are as absent from our feature films as Black and Hispanic faces were from our television screens in the early Sixties. Where are the stories of our ethnic minorities? Our underclasses? Where is the wisdom of our elders? Someone else has an agenda, too.

I hate to write. It hurts. I avoid it at all costs. But eventually, all this gets me into my seat. I don't mean to be self-righteous, but without this awareness, I would have given up long ago. I am rejected, criticized, rewritten. And I keep going. I compromise to get things made. And I refuse to compromise when the reason for starting is no longer evident. Because it's not about me. It's about what needs to get out there. It's about the story finding its real ending in the effect it has on the world.

*Sesame Street* changed our culture. And it changed me. Nothing "grown up" I've ever done will have a greater effect. I'm proud of where I began. And when I lose heart and think I can't do it one more time, fight one more battle, I remember where I learned to write.

# Bill Boulware

## The New Guy

---

*"And make no mistake, even though there has been a tremendous amount of progress, the need to diversify is as great as ever."*

Bill Boulware grew tired of the long form after writing *Gone with the Wind, Casablanca* and *Citizen Kane* and began to write sitcoms. After co-creating *227*, he's been a writer-producer on *The Fresh Prince of Bel-Air, In the House, The Parkers, One on One* and a host of shows you've never heard of, or from the ratings, never watched.

All the talk of diversity these days has put me in mind of my first staff job. I had come to Los Angeles to write dramatic movies; but after four years of limited success—meaning, I was doing clerical work to make ends meet—I decided to try my hand at sitcoms. Thanks to a friend (Who else? You certainly didn't expect me to say "agent"?), I got the opportunity to pitch to the ABC show *Benson*, which starred Robert Guillaume. The show had been on two seasons and was a hit for the network. In hopes of getting a freelance script, which would have enabled me to add a fifth food group to my meager meals, I pitched five story ideas and of course left my "spec" (for *Love Sydney*, if anyone remembers that!). The producers liked three of my ideas and told me they would get back to me after they ran them by ABC. That was on a Friday. The following Monday they called and offered me a staff position on the show. I was almost there before they hung up the phone.

Although it wasn't called diversity at the time, I was hired because the star of the show, Robert Guillaume, insisted on having an African-American writer on staff. If he hadn't, my days of Xeroxing would have undoubtedly been prolonged. This is not to say that the only reason I was hired was because I'm black—without some expression of potential or talent, it wouldn't have occurred— but rather it was a function of the desire to diversify. In order to sincerely meet this goal, the parties concerned took the time to make it a priority. I joined the staff a month into their production.

The first day on the job, I sat nervously in my office fighting the urge to gravitate to the Xerox room. After some time, I stepped out into the hallway to discover an empty office. No writers, assistants, or producers—the entire place was deserted. I wasn't quite sure what to make of it. I wondered if perhaps there had been some kind of fire drill, although I thought they only did that in school. I searched the other floors of the building and although Sunset Gower was, at the time, not a busy lot, there were people in the building. When I inquired if they perhaps knew where I might find, well, anyone—they suggested I try the stage. Not wanting to show my ignorance I simply said thanks, then wandered around the lot looking for "the stage." Finally, I gave up and returned to the office. Eventually everyone returned and I discovered they were at the table read. No one had remembered to tell me; they simply had forgotten I was there.

Fortunately, that was not a harbinger of things to come. The producers and the company were all supportive of me and I remained for three seasons, eventually moving up to Executive Story Editor. Yet many writers of color remain the forgotten people, even once through the door. On subsequent shows I worked, it was not unusual to see other African-American writers isolated and shunted aside, even on a show that I co-created but did not run. In many cases, the producers felt the writers were foisted on them by actors and, as such, prejudged those writers. My case was different and I attribute that to being chosen directly by the producers of the show. Hopefully, that will be the case in future efforts to diversify shows. And make no mistake, even though there has been a tremendous amount of progress, the need to diversify is as great as ever. Opportunities for writers of color have been restricted primarily to "Black" shows, creating a sort of de facto segregation. In almost 20 years of employment, I have never been on a show where either the cast or the lead character was not black. This has not been by design, but rather the result of the opportunities afforded me. Whereas I am grateful to be employed, it is discouraging to feel restricted, both for economic as well as creative reasons. To limit my expression to a certain milieu or to suggest that my experience is so narrow that it cannot incorporate a culture in which I am as much a part as any white writer is the height of conceit. I have been in rooms where white writers asked in veiled terms how someone black might express a term, but I have never heard a black writer ask how someone white would say something. Living in both worlds, we know how. Despite this, it is white writers who have been able to move between "black" shows and "white" shows, while it remains a rarity for black writers. This will only change if those in a position of power make an effort to do so. And if change does come about, someone remember the new guy in the office.

# Bruce Joel Rubin

## Script Advice From Beyond The Grave

*"My son Joshua was about to have the first peanut butter and jelly Bar Mitzvah in all of Los Angeles and was spared that humiliation by my sale of the script."*

Bruce Joel Rubin is the author of three motion pictures, *Jacob's Ladder*, *My Life* and *Ghost*, for which he won an Oscar® for best original screenplay. He has also co-written *Deep Impact*, *Stuart Little 2*, *Brainstorm* (original story credit), *Deceived* (for which he used a pseudonym), and *Deadly Friend*.

In the spring of 1984, my wife Blanche quit her job at Northern Illinois University, put our house on the market, and announced we were moving to Hollywood. She knew I would die if I did not pursue my dream of becoming a screenwriter. That June, we arrived in Los Angeles with our two young sons and enough money to live for two months if we were frugal. Robert M. Sherman, a producer friend, called me soon after with a possible screenwriting job, adapting a novel called *Friend*. It was a bizarre story about a young boy who builds a robot. The boy's next-door neighbor is a teenage girl he is secretly in love with, who is badly treated by her abusive father. One day, the father throws her down a flight of stairs and she is pronounced brain dead at the hospital. In despair, the boy decides to do brain surgery on the young girl using his robot's brain to bring her back to life. To his astonishment and ours, he succeeds. Unfortunately, the girl comes back as a crazy person and goes around killing all the people who have done her wrong. I turned the job down, certain that I had not come to Hollywood to write stuff like this. I'd rather starve.

The next morning, I was sitting and meditating as I do every morning. As I observed my wandering mind, I could see that I was still feeling smug about walking away from the project and proud that I was maintaining my integrity in Hollywood. At that very moment I heard a voice, the voice of my meditation teacher Rudi, who had died 11 years before. Calling through the ether he yelled, "Schmuck! There is more integrity in feeding your family than in turning down jobs." He then insisted that I get up from my cross-legged position, go to the phone, and call the producer. It was 7:00 in the morning and I thought too early to call anyone, but then again, I don't often get directives from beyond the grave. So I hobbled to the telephone, woke the producer, and lied that I had found a way to make this a worthy film and would like the job. He said he was delighted and I was hired.

Then, extraordinary things began to happen. I worked very hard to give the script some human dimension and when I finished, a vice president at Warner Bros. called me. She said she was amazed that the script had made her cry. I was amazed, too. The movie attracted Wes Craven as the director and it was a delight to work with him. While the movie was shooting, I was able to bring my wife and boys to the Warner's lot and we all luxuriated in the excitement of being in the movie business. Ari, my youngest son (he was 5 then), became a mascot on the set. He fell in love with Kristy Swanson, who played the girl next door, and she was sweet enough to recognize his adoration and take him on his first date, to McDonald's. He is now 24 and has never forgotten it.

Unfortunately, when the movie previewed for a Wes Craven audience, they hated it. They had not come for an emotional experience and the panicked studio brass decided that we needed to put in more gore, six more scenes to be exact, each bloodier than the one before. We did and at the next preview the audience was propelled out of its seats, literally standing on top of them, screaming with unbridled excitement and blood lust. They especially liked the old lady who had been decapitated by a basketball, running headless through her house spouting torrents of blood from her neck. Not surprisingly, the film was given an X rating for excessive horror. With each horrific frame that was cut from the movie, Wes said we were losing another million dollars at the box office. It turns out that the film only made about $9 million, so you can imagine how many frames were cut.

I was pretty ashamed of the final product and wondered why my teacher had journeyed from the netherworld to encourage me to do it. But there is a happy ending, actually a few happy endings. Because the film got made, I got a bonus and that bonus was the down payment on our house. My son Joshua was about to have the first peanut butter and jelly Bar Mitzvah in all of Los Angeles and was spared that humiliation by my sale of the script. And finally, a year later, in the fourth month of a horrible writer's strike when my bank account had dwindled to $400 and we were fearful of losing our home, I got my first residual check for what was now called *Deadly Friend*. I looked at it, saw $3,500 and was wide-eyed with excitement. I kept thanking Rudi, my teacher, for making me take this job. Then my wife looked at the check and gasped. She told me that I had miscounted the zeros. It was actually $35,000. *Deadly Friend* had saved our lives.

There is a moral to this tale. Don't turn down jobs in Hollywood. Take whatever the universe offers gratefully and then do your best work. You might also try meditating. It couldn't hurt.

# Gregory Allen Howard

## Hello, I'm Larry...

*"I was spraying words; more specifically, scripts. I was a fucking machine."*

Gregory Allen Howard is a playwright-screenwriter. His produced credits include *Glory Road, Remember The Titans, Ali* (story credit only, thank God), some really shitty, half-assed sitcoms, the play *Tinseltown Trilogy* and numerous articles and essays. But most of all, he's a survivor—a creative cockroach who refuses to pleasure his enemies by being killed.

Feedback. It's the one thing a writer longs for in the beginning. From anyone or *anything*. When I started out, the lack of this almost destroyed my initial attempts at becoming a screenwriter.

Circa 1987. I was living in the delightful, ethnically rich and crime-ridden Rampart neighborhood of Los Angeles, having just moved out from back East. I was determined to become a screenwriter. I had no idea the *challenges*—yeah, right—that lay ahead. I just knew I had discovered this *thing* inside me that demanded to get out.

I took a telemarketing job because it: a) would pay my modest bills; and b) was a job that I could leave and not have to think about after I left. Five hours at night, five nights a week. But I was free all day.

And all day I wrote. Like a demon.

As I indicated, one day the muse just visited me. The day before, I couldn't crap out a single word. The next day, it was a fire hose I couldn't turn off. I was spraying *words*; more specifically, *scripts*. I was a fucking machine. Not to put too fine a point on this, but I was like a young boy who discovered his thingy was for something other than pissing. Baby, I was doing it *all* the time.

And the scripts just kept piling up.

Once I had a heap, I then started spending my time *marketing* because that's really what new writers have to do unless they're really connected (and some of these pricks are, but I'm not *that* jealous of them… at least not anymore). In the circle of people I've met in this business, I'm the only one who had not one single contact. Not even a name. Nada.

So I got the agency list and started submitting to the agents and agencies that would accept unsolicited scripts. And yes, boys and girls, I turned into a goddamn stalker of agents, managers and assistants—*anybody* who was in Castle Hollywood. It was nothing to send a script to an agent and call 50 times in a week. Sometimes, 20 times in a day. In a year and a half, I probably made 3 or 4 *thousand* calls to agents and others. And I was still writing when I wasn't harassing.

In the entirety of that year and a half, not a single agent returned a single phone call. Not one. I could not get any feedback. And that lack of oxygen was starting to kill me, kill my spirit. I was doubly disappointed because I thought the comedies

(I was out of my element, but I had no idea what my element was) that I was cranking out were as funny as the stuff I was watching on the screen. Hell, I thought my comedies were *better*.

But the fact that no one would *tell* me anything was making me crazy. I felt my life force begin to drain from my body. No one's ever gonna help me. No one's ever gonna talk to me. All I needed was for someone to say something—*anything*—about the work I was producing. I needed to know *why* I wasn't breaking through with the stuff I was writing.

In those days, when I got depressed (a near daily occurrence), I often would get three Tommy's Burgers (right down the street from me) and go to the Universal multiplex around 11 a.m. and sit through three movies (sometimes four if my ass could take it). This day it was three. Movies then and now were a palliative for me—a cheap means of escape to other worlds (which is why I love movies).

I got home near 7 p.m. When I walked in, I had a message. I played it. "Hello, I'm Larry. I read a couple of your scripts… they're good…" To this day, that call may be the most important thing that has happened to me because I was ready to quit—give up.

"Larry" was a reader for Melinda Jason, a one-time powerful agent-turned-producer. Just out of Harvard, he himself had Hollywood dreams beyond being a reader. Why he picked my half-assed comedies and called me, to this day, remains a mystery. Maybe it shows he had no taste in his early days in town. Maybe he sensed my desperation.

We talked. Had lunch. Became friends. He told me: "They're funny, really funny, but the ideas behind the scripts are thin. There's no hook." That's all I needed to hear. If *that* was the only problem, then I could overcome that easily. I'd just keep working.

And, unfortunately for my new friend, I returned to writing renewed and full of vigor. Seventeen scripts in 18 months. And I made that poor bastard read every single one.

Nothing ever came of any of those scripts. I changed course and started writing drama and, the rest, as they say, is history. But because Larry gave me hope, light, *feedback*, I didn't quit and kept plugging.

And that is my Hollywood screenwriting story.

P.S. "Larry" eventually became Lawrence Guterman, the award-winning director of *Cats & Dogs* and my best friend.

# Henry Bromell

## Nobody Knows Anything[1]

---

*"Coincidence and karma? That pretty much sums it up."*

Henry Bromell wrote, directed and executive produced the acclaimed Showtime movie *Last Call*. He has written and produced the TV dramas *Northern Exposure*, *I'll Fly Away*, *Homicide: Life on the Street* and *Chicago Hope*. He has won two Peabody Awards, a Writers Guild Award, a Humanitas Prize and two O. Henry Awards for fiction.

Many years ago, not long after my son was born, my wife, Trish Soodik, gainfully employed and highly paid as a TV comedy writer, announced that she was quitting TV and its insanely grueling hours in order to actually see this aforementioned son of ours. I was, at the time, a freelance screenwriter. I rarely got assignments and, when I did, they were pretty stupid. I wrote original scripts, at least one a year, and sold them, only to find myself being ordered by studios and producers to systematically destroy them. I needed steady employment and smarter bosses. Ironically, I turned to TV, as my wife had done before me. I went

---

1. Thanks to William Goldman's *Adventures in the Screen Trade* for this terse—and accurate—assessment of the collective wisdom of Hollywood.

---

looking for work on TV dramas. I met some nice people but got no work. Then one day, the phone rang and a voice asked me if I was I. I said I was. The voice introduced itself as John Falsey and then asked me to lunch. "I've got a story to tell you," said John Falsey. I had no idea that John Falsey was one half of the TV writing/producing team Brand/Falsey. I just like a good mystery.

I showed up for lunch, in Westwood, and met there a slender Irishman grinning at me from behind 17 layers of self-protective Irish charm. He was like a beautifully polished veneer. We sat and he told me his story, which went something like this:

Years earlier, John Falsey, a young and struggling writer, applied to the Iowa Writers Workshop, where I was at the time employed as a Visiting Writer. John had read and enjoyed a number of my stories in *The New Yorker* and somehow knew I was teaching at Iowa. Anyway, he didn't get in. Indignant, he called up the Workshop and demanded to know why he had been rejected. "Well, it's harder to get in here than Harvard, you shouldn't feel bad—" "Yeah, but did Henry Bromell read my stuff?" Falsey asked. As if he knew me, right? As if I would be personally upset if I found out John Falsey had been rejected by the Iowa Writers Workshop. The Irish. Of which I am one, by the way.

So anyway, it turned out I hadn't read his stuff, and I should have. He was told to call back Monday. Meanwhile, I did read John Falsey's writing, and then I wrote a memo saying the Iowa Writers Workshop not only should accept John Falsey, they should give him money. Which they did. When John showed up that autumn, I had moved on, so we didn't meet, but he had filched my memo from his file and kept it tacked to the wall next to his writing desk for all these years…

John Falsey sat back and smiled his Irish smile. "I've always wanted to thank you. So, thank you."

"You're welcome," I said.

Now, the truth is that I had no memory of reading John's work or writing that memo. But I was pleased with what I had apparently done. My younger self sounded noble and plucky.

"Is there anything I can do for you?" John sweetly inquired.

"Well," I said. "I don't know. I don't think so. What do you do?"

"I make TV dramas."

I had a moment's severe confusion.

"How did you know I was looking for work in TV drama?" I asked.

His turn to be confused. Because he didn't know.

So… coincidence?

I explained to him that I was, in fact, looking for a TV job.

"My partner Josh and I are starting a new show for CBS called *Northern Exposure*," he announced. "Wanna work on that?"

"Sure."

Sure.

He took me over to meet Josh Brand, who clearly thought his partner had taken leave of his senses. Josh paced back and forth like Groucho Marx, worried as hell. Hire a TV writer who had never written TV? But he slowly succumbed to John Falsey's narrative of his and my relationship, which I could see was starting to assume mythic proportions in Falsey's perfervid imagination.

Plus, Josh liked my stories, when he read them later.

And so I got a job writing TV drama, thus beginning what turned out to be almost 15 years of pain and pleasure and a steady check in the S & M Palace known as Network TV.

So... karma?

Coincidence and karma?

That pretty much sums it up.

# Rosemary Anne Sisson

## A Chateau in Hollywood

*"I was blissfully billeted behind the lines in a Chateau."*

Rosemary Anne Sisson's first three television plays went out live, only to vanish forever with the credits. She continued with contributions to *The Six Wives of Henry VIII*, *Elizabeth R.* and *Upstairs, Downstairs*, and is pleased to also have written for *The Young Indiana Jones* and *Murder, She Wrote*. She wrote or co-wrote five films for Disney, as well as eleven novels and nine stage plays.

Frank Paris was Story Editor for Walt Disney Productions and my agent had recommended me to him for a film based on a classic English novel. Over lunch in London, I told him what I had done and what I hoped to do, but confessed that I had never yet written a film. Some weeks later, he telephoned to tell me that the rights to the book had fallen through.

"But I won't forget you," he said.

Ho yus! I thought, in my best Cockney. That's the last I'll hear of that!

But I was wrong. Five years later, he telephoned me to say that

Disney had acquired the rights to an Australian story and that he felt I was right for it.

I don't remember much more until I was in the Chateau Marmont, gazing out at the lights of Los Angeles and hearing the police sirens whooping up and down the Hollywood Hills. ("She calls it a Chateau," remarked Larry Clemmons, who wrote the scripts for *The Jungle Book*, *The Aristocats* and *The Rescuers*. "It's a rooming house on Sunset Boulevard!") It is true that the Chateau then was distinctly rundown but very comfortable and suited English people perfectly. The kitchen dated from the 1920s and the receptionist was like Zazu Pitts. When I asked if anyone famous was staying there, she would vaguely leaf through the reservation pages.

"Um—Hermione Baddeley," she would murmur. "Myrna Loy..."

My apartment had once been Jean Harlow's, and I was in Hollywood to write a film.

Mind, I was not completely naïve. Even before I left England, I had remarked to Frank, "I suppose I have to write for a particular Star?"

"Certainly not," he had replied. "Disney is the Star. We get the script right first, and then we cast it, but the most important thing is the script."

"These," I thought, "are my sort of people!"

There were, of course, one or two things to sort out. Disney's working day began at about 7.30 a.m. and by 5.30 p.m. the car park was empty. But years of University teaching meant that I was happy to make corrections during the day, or to do research—especially in the Disney library where, in my honor, they had been kind enough to institute the custom of afternoon tea. However, my writing brain didn't come to life until around 8 p.m. The answer was to provide me with a second typewriter at the Chateau, but even so, my lack of visible activity at the Studio caused a certain amount of anxiety, especially to Frank. It was even worse when, seeing that my first obligation was to provide an Outline, I merrily dashed off ten pages, sent them along to Frank's office, leapt into my beloved Mustang and drove away.

Frank rang me at the Chateau, and I knew from his voice that there was something wrong.

"You don't like it!" I exclaimed, astonished.

"Listen," he said. "I know what you're going to write, and you know what you're going to write, but Disney will say, 'You mean we brought this woman all the way from England for this?'"

I saw his point. After some gin and tonic bought at Greenblatt's and a pork chop from Ralph's Supermarket, I sat down and typed a 20-page outline so complete that they could almost have sent me home at once. Fortunately, they didn't, and so began five years of joyful commuting between *Upstairs, Downstairs* in London and Disney films in Los Angeles, with directors like Don Chaffey, Charles Jarrott and Norman Tokar and actors who included Helen Hayes, Alastair Sim, David Niven, Bette Davis and a magical young actress called Jodie Foster.

I always regretted not meeting Walt Disney, who had just died, but I did later learn that his relations with the Writers Guild were not always entirely happy, and instead, I had the good fortune of working with his son-in-law, Ron Miller.

"Can I ask a silly question?" Ron would say, mildly. "How did they know that?" or "Can I ask a silly question? Why didn't they do that sooner?"

"Ron," I said to him once, "I don't like your silly questions. They always mean ten pages of rewrites."

To this day, I may not win Oscars®, but I defy anyone to find a weak point in my storytelling.

This was supposed to be a tale from the Hollywood trenches, and I promise faithfully that since then, I have done my share of trudging in the mud, and more than once have been shot in the back. But even a foot-slogging soldier now and then strikes it lucky, and just for once I wasn't in the trenches. I was blissfully billeted behind the lines in a Chateau.

# Margot Black

## Chin Up; Tits Out

---

*"I spend the next 14 hours with my cell phone in the back room at Circle K hovering over the fax machine."*

Margot Black is a writer/comedian/babe who has performed stand-up comedy for over a decade. Her writing has appeared in *Written By, She's So Funny* and *Joke Soup.* Currently writing for Disney, she enjoys doing it for money.

Writing television had been my goal for lifetimes. Trees died, scripts stacked up on my shelves. I couldn't get a foot in the door, but at least I'd given myself a fair shot at carpal tunnel syndrome. Then one day it hit me: "I know, I'll create my own television show."

Sitting on a friend's floor, I scribble the outline for a comedy game show called *Stinkin' Rich: A Celebration of Blatant, Garish and Ostentatious Consumerism* on the back of a Chinese food takeout bag. I made a list of everyone I knew in Hollywood (that includes the Daily Grill waiter who once slipped me his tongue and his phone number) and called them. Daily Grill waiter's sister's husband got me my first meeting.

The cable Development Woman says, "*Stinkin' Rich* is hilarious but we're not looking for a game show." Development Woman refers me to three other people. I meet those people, they refer me to other people, who refer me to other people—and then one of those other people's people makes me an offer. Not a big offer, but an offer. Heck, I don't even understand the offer, but I got it in writing. Oh-My-God!!! I got an offer!

My inner car salesman kicks into high gear. I call everyone back that I met with and tell them I got an offer. I get three more offers.

I call a Mega Manager I met filming a Comedy Central short in a meat locker. Mega Manager refers me to a Big Barracuda Lawyer and another potential partner. Big Barracuda Lawyer's shoes cost more than my mortgage. He takes me on. I meet the other Potential Partner at her compound. Potential Partner has a husband, an ex-husband, an assistant, a nanny, two kids, two cars, a pool and a guest house. I have a boy friend and a manila folder with four offers.

My folder and I meet the only Big Wig Agent who will schedule a meeting that decade. Big Wig listens to my show and laughs. Big belly laughs. He wants to be my agent. I run to the car to call my dad and screeeeeeeeeam into the phone.

Potential Partner turns into my actual partner. Big Wig brings in a junior agent. We travel to all our meetings together—a wave of Armani suits and me. Holy shit, I have a posse!

Three black BMWs and a ten-year-old green Saab pull into a midsized production company specializing in syndication (Syndication! There's a kidney-shaped swimming pool in my future)! We pitch, and Syndication Man makes an offer. We schedule an appointment with a Big Network. Big Agency decides it's best to tell Syndication Man. Syndication Man says, "If you don't take me into that meeting and include me, I'll pull out and leave you with nothing." *What!?* Can he do that?

We tell Big Network about Syndication Man and get an

additional offer from Big Network. I call my dad and tell him while I surf the net for private islands. Two days later, Big Network rescinds Big Offer, stating they have a Big Clash with another Big Show and Big Agency is pissed—Big Time!

We go back to Syndication Man and get a step deal to mount three staged run-throughs of the game show. My partner, however, simultaneously accepts a job as an executive producer of a long-running daily television show and my project becomes one of her extracurricular affairs.

My partner has no time for me but, apparently, has time to have drinks with everyone we are working with. I have no idea who is wagging what, but meetings happen without me and my phone calls aren't getting returned. She tries to squeeze me out of the show. I'm completely confused and have no idea how the tide has turned. A friend of mine gives me a copy of *What Makes Sammy Run*. I read it in the bathtub and cry.

My partner and I each get to stage a run-through. I go first. Syndication Man is out of town but Big Wig Agent comes and Syndication's Right Hand Man is there. I get, "That's great. Could you punch up the third act a bit?" My partner and her husband are ill-prepared for their run-through. Syndication Man attends this one. I cringe as I watch from the side, not sure if I want to vomit or take hostages. They run through a 24-minute show in under 15 minutes. The notes come back, "We love the title but don't like the show." There is no third run-through.

Big Wig walks me to my car and I burst into tears. "I'll find you a new partner," he says. I construct a shrine to him in my living room.

I go back to part-time work and practicing kinetic control over inanimate objects ("ring, damn phone, ring!"). A couple of months later, Big Wig calls me at 9:30 p.m. "I just met a development woman at a cocktail party. There's a new network being announced, they're in town looking for product. I got you an appointment tomorrow at 10 a.m., they're leaving for New York at three—can you do it?"

Big Wig brings a New Junior agent to the meeting. I pitch the show and in the room they say, "YES!!!!" New Network Woman asks me if I could deliver the pilot within five weeks; they need it for some cable announcement thingy. I really have no idea what she said; all I heard was, "Yes." I look over at Big Wig and he gives me a subtle nod. I say, "Sure, no problem."

No problem my ass. Next week is Christmas. "Congratulations, Slugger, you hit a home run!" Big Wig says, adorably giddy as he hands me the name and phone number of the vacation villa he'll be in with his family for the next two weeks.

New Junior Agent Man becomes my go-to guy. I'm his first deal, it's my first show, he's got production experience and a sense of humor—we get along great. He introduces me to several new partners and at 4 pm, Christmas Eve, I find one that fits. New Partner will be able to start working with me the second week of January. We toast our new partnership with eggnog lattes.

I have reason to celebrate. I got a license-fee deal. I'm not sure exactly what it is. A year ago, my greatest showbiz concern was, could I sell tee shirts after a performance? Now my fine print has fine print.

Big Barracuda Lawyer tells me I won't be profitable to him under this arrangement. He dumps me in the middle of contract negotiations. My deal can't close. I stick pins in my voodoo doll and add "find new lawyer" to my two-thousand-page "to do" list.

My boyfriend and I plan to spend part of the holidays visiting my parents in their brand-new home at the bottom of a National Park. It's a 10-mile drive to the nearest human. We get there and they have one phone line, no fax. I pay the guy at the local Circle K $25 bucks a day to receive faxes.

I spend the vacation week in my dad's home talking to New Junior Agent Man at his mom's home. My agent explains I still don't have much of anything until I can secure my talent. I need a Beverly Hills-Type Female Guest Star and a Rich Man Celebrity Announcer. And I need them yesterday.

My first L.A. Landlord used to walk dogs for a Beverly Hills female celebrity. I call her, and she tells me she has the dogs right now—Beverly Hills Female Celebrity is on vacation in Costa Rica. I fax L.A. Landlord the script, she reads it, calls Costa Rica and Beverly Hills-Female Celebrity agrees to read show. I fax script to Costa Rica. My parents' phone rings in the middle of the night— Costa Rica calling. Beverly Hills Female Celebrity would like to participate. "How much does it pay?" she asks. My meager budget sounds insulting, but I realize it would sound much better as a Gucci shopping spree. "It pays a Gucci shopping spree *and* a limo will pick you up. You'll be my first guest if I get picked up and you'll have my unending gratitude forever." Beverly Hills Female Celebrity cuts her vacation short and returns to Los Angeles to do my pilot.

I know a Rich Celebrity Announcer Man's Agent in New York from the stand-up world. His client is in Anguilla. I e-mail him the script and he forwards it to his client. I get a two-word fax from Rich Celebrity Man in Anguilla, "I'm in." I call back his agent and negotiate the terms. I spend the next 14 hours with my cell phone in the back room at Circle K hovering over the fax machine. The clerk and owner take to checking on me periodically, "Hey, Showbiz, eat something." By 11:30 p.m. the next night, the talent deals are done. I got a show. My dad, stepmom and boyfriend bring champagne and caviar for everyone. We turn up the music, drink and dance to disco at the Circle K.

New Partner returns to town. We shoot the pilot, deliver it on time, and get announced at the cable thingy as the Top Five Picks for Pick-up.

I find a new lawyer and three months, six trees and ten million faxes later, my deal closes.

A month later, they test the pilot. I get a call from my Big Wig Agent, "Testing was okay, but the network has decided to change direction and won't be needing it." "Are we going to try again?" I ask. Big Wig says, "No. We did this one. Let's do a new one." Simple as that. It's over. Later that night, close to crying in my Margarita, Seasoned Professional Female Friend counsels, "Don't worry, you'll do it again. Chin up; tits out."

There's a T.S. Eliot quote on my refrigerator that says, "Only those who risk going too far can find out how far one can go."

I recently helped someone else write and sell their first show. I watched him go through the eye of his hurricane and wanted to hold him in the fetal position and say, "It's okay, I know the pain, I know the fear, I know the responsibility." But it's not possible. It's part of the process, part of the deal. His pilot aired but didn't get picked up. "Hey," I tried to cheer him up, "You got on the air. Your first failure was better than my first failure." He gives me a hug as he hands me my last check. I'm halfway out the door and I remember to tell him, "Don't worry, you'll do it again."

I think of Seasoned Professional Female Friend and T.S. Eliot, and walk to the bank with my chin up and my tits out.

# Robert Nelson Jacobs

## Universe Number Two

---

*"But that script, conceived on a gurney in the emergency room and born five years later, did exactly what it was supposed to do."*

Robert Nelson Jacobs was nominated for an Academy Award®, a Writers Guild Award and a BAFTA Award for his adapted screenplay *Chocolat*. His other produced screenplays include *The Shipping News*, *Dinosaur* and *Out to Sea*.

You never know when an idea for a screenplay will hit you.

In 1988, when I was a young, unproduced screenwriter, a speeding car struck me in a crosswalk on Ocean Avenue in Santa Monica. Several eyewitnesses later told me they had been certain I'd died at the moment of impact.

I arrived at the emergency room with multiple fractures and contusions—but miraculously, no permanent damage.

Lying in the ER in a state of shock, I thought to myself: it makes no sense that I'm still alive. And then I vaguely recalled a theory I'd once read in a layman's book on particle physics: that certain cataclysmic moments in time can split the universe into two alternate universes. (At least that's how I remembered the theory.) I suddenly experienced a daydream whose clarity bordered on hallucination. I imagined that the universe had split in two at the moment the car had struck me—and that in one universe I had died instantly, while in the other universe I'd survived. I thought: *What if my wife, mourning my untimely death in Universe #1, somehow found out that I am alive here in Universe #2?*

Then I decided I was thirsty and asked the nurse for a Diet Coke.

Five years later, in 1993, my career as a screenwriter appeared to be over. I had been writing with a partner, a talented guy with whom I'd landed a few low-level development deals... but nothing had ever been produced. And the phone was now silent and cold. And when I ran into my agent at a party, he failed to recognize me, though he admitted I looked familiar. And the term "young writer" no longer applied.

My wife Hilary and I discussed the possibility of my getting a real job. I picked up a brochure on how to become a real estate salesperson. I grew somber and started ruminating about death... and my morbid reverie led me back to the weird daydream I'd had in the ER in '88.

I began outlining a story about a lonely woman in her 30s who lost her fiancé in a car crash ten years earlier. Through a supernatural intervention (don't ask), the woman is transported to an alternate universe in which the guy is alive, and she's married to him, and their life is a suburban nightmare, replete with bratty kids, extramarital affairs, a septic tank and a 30-year mortgage.

I told Hilary my story idea and we agreed I should give screenwriting one last shot; she'd continue paying the bills for a few more months while I hammered out a spec script.

It was a feverish time. I started waking up at 4 a.m. every morning (spontaneously, without an alarm clock) and wrote with an urgency (no, a desperation) that I had never experienced before.

A few months later, I held in my hands a finished script titled *Worlds Apart*.

I delivered it to my agent's office. He remembered my name, which I took as a good sign. But he did not respond to the script.

I started sending *Worlds Apart* to other agents. One by one, they passed. Five different agents, five different ways to say no.

Then an agent named Frank Wuliger said yes. That's when the real anxiety began.

Frank sent out the script to producers on a Wednesday. At 5 p.m., Thursday evening, we got a real live offer. The kind of offer I had previously only read about in *Daily Variety*. The six-figure kind. But the offer was "pre-emptive": if I didn't say yes by 11 p.m., the offer would be null and void.

Here I was, an unemployed writer in a small apartment with a hard-working wife and an infant son. Plus, my Toyota Corolla really, really needed a new muffler. After a brief, giddy deliberation, I called Frank to say I'd take the deal.

But the plot, he informed me, had thickened. Other producers, including some real heavyweights, were now excited about the script. They were *begging* that I wait until tomorrow to sell it. "Why tomorrow?" I wondered. "Why don't these 'heavyweights' bid on the script tonight, if they're so damned excited?" Frank explained that these producers were not "buyers." They had to give the script to the studios—the guys who could actually write the check—so that they could read it on Friday.

With the kind of buzz this script was generating, Frank said, we might sell it for a million dollars—if I could just bite the bullet and decline the pre-emptive offer already on the table.

"This is a poker game," Frank told me, "and my gut says we're holding four aces." Buoyed by Frank's confidence and dizzied by the adrenaline now surging through my body, I declined the pre-emptive offer.

I looked out the window and the stars in the cloudless sky appeared unnaturally dazzling and precise. I felt brave, decisive, intensely alive.

At 4 a.m., I am kneeling next to the toilet, riding wave after wave of anxiety-driven nausea. I have not slept. Maybe I will never sleep again.

What in God's name have I done? How could I so brazenly gamble with my family's future? I am greedy, impulsive, vain. I am a fool.

Hilary wakes up and tries to reassure me, but she sees the panic glittering in my eyes and knows I'm beyond her reach.

I experience a vivid fantasy: Once again, the universe has split in two. In one universe, I have said yes to the pre-emptive offer, and Hilary and I are sharing a bottle of champagne in the bathtub. But in this universe—the universe in which I've moronically said no to the offer—I am gripping the toilet, saying Kaddish in memory of my shattered aspirations.

The next morning, the phone does not ring. I keep checking to make sure it's plugged into the wall. By 10:30 a.m., I can stand it no longer and I call Frank to see if there's any news. Not a peep, he calmly informs me.

"But someone *will* make an offer, right?" I plead.

"Who knows?" he observes philosophically.

The hours drain away. At 1 p.m., Frank calls to say a major studio executive wants to have a "creative discussion" with me prior to making an offer.

I hurriedly call the executive and he proceeds to give me the most idiotic and perverse creative notes I have ever heard—notes which, if executed, would annihilate the emotional logic of the script. I take a deep breath—momentarily suspended in the delicate balance between art and commerce—and then I say only that his notes are "truly amazing." Flattered, he promises we'll talk later in the day.

I never hear from him, or his studio, again.

At 2:30, Friday afternoon, I am dancing on the edge of sanity— dramatically sashaying around the apartment and scat-singing be-bop solos in the style of Charlie Parker. Hilary is very worried. She calls a friend to "just come hang out with us," as she carefully puts it. I suspect it is actually a suicide watch.

At 3:00, Frank calls to say we just got an offer on the script, but it was a tad lower than the one we got last night—so he turned it down. "What?!" I scream.

"This is a poker game," he reminds me. "We cannot show weakness."

By 5:30, Friday afternoon, bids have come in from three different companies—and thank God, one of them matches last night's pre-emptive offer. And the executive is someone I know and trust. So I can relax, right?

"But wait!" Frank enthuses, "Just listen to this!" He recites a long list of Heavy Hitters who are begging to read my script over the weekend, so they can bid it up into the stratosphere on

Monday morning.

"Is it possible the current offer will evaporate over the weekend?" I ask.

"Anything's possible," he says. "But if we wait, you could hit the jackpot."

I am, however, a slightly wiser (and much older) man than I was last night.

"Frank," I say, "I've *already* hit the jackpot."

He doesn't argue. Not a word. He gets it.

*Worlds Apart* never got produced, though it came awfully close. In the years since, several movies with similar themes (*Sliding Doors, The Family Man, Me Myself & I*) have appeared, making it virtually impossible that *Worlds Apart* will ever make the leap to the screen.

But that script, conceived on a gurney in the emergency room and born five years later, did exactly what it was supposed to do. It delivered me into a strange, hospitable universe where I'm permitted to write screenplays for a living, a world in which it's been years since anyone has asked me when I'm going to get a real job.

# Marc Norman

## The Best Thing To Say For It

---

*"He put us through all that to get his name in the paper."*

Marc Norman won two Oscars®, two Golden Globes, the WGA Best Screenplay and several other awards for the screenplay of *Shakespeare in Love* (co-written with Tom Stoppard). He currently lives in Santa Monica with his wife. His two kids moved out, but one has moved back.

Sometimes it's best to have the worst thing that will ever happen to you in the entire sweep of your movie industry career happen early. I didn't read this someplace. It happened to me.

The situation is this—it's 1967, I've spent my life growing up in L.A., I've always been curious, even aroused, by what goes on behind all those studio walls I see out the window of my mom's car as we drive past, all that sex and power and fun. Now I'm 27, I'm living in West Hollywood in a rundown Nathaniel-Westish bungalow court, 65 bucks a month. I've just written my first screenplay over a long, scorching summer sitting in my kitchen sweating in my underwear. Now it's done and I'm dreaming of where it will all lead.

First, to a young agent at a small agency, who shops the screenplay around. Nobody buys it, but I get a few small jobs, some days, a week, here and there, patching episode TV scripts. In general, I'm happy.

Then the agent calls—*mirabile dictu*, he's gotten me a job writing a screenplay. No. Yes! A screenplay—a real movie! For Columbia, 12 weeks guaranteed, half-a-thousand dollars a week. Something about film students.

"You were a film student, right?" he asks me as I caper around my living room. The truth is, I tell him, no. "Well, say you were," he says.

I go to Columbia—this is old Columbia, on Gower—and it turns out it's all true. The producer is a guy named David Swift— he's got close-cut white hair, a lean look. He was an animator at Disney—now he's producing features, has just had a minor hit with something called *The Interns*, a low-budget slice-of-life thing, young interns at a hospital; their individual stories. Film schools are in the news these days, even on the cover of *Time*—remember this is '67, high-water New Wave, people are actually using the word "cinema" in daily conversations. So *The Interns* with film students is what he's after. And not only that, his idea is that film students write the script. And he tells me he's hired two more film students as production assistants—it's a film student extravaganza.

"You were a film student?" he asks me as I'm leaving. Once again, jerk that I am, I tell him no. "Don't tell anybody that," he warns me.

He pairs me with another writer, Diana Gould, who actually is a bona fide film student from UCLA. Somebody shows us our offices—they turn out to be dressing rooms, hers left over from some '50s bombshell contract actress, mine less distinguished, but it has a barber chair you can play around with. Are we insulted at the shabby quarters? C'mon—we're thrilled, we're in a studio, behind the walls (she's got the same fantasies I have), getting paid, working on a Hollywood movie. Talk about fulfillment.

Of course, now we have to write it, and we have no real idea how to do that, but we talk it over and come up with a plan—we'll dream up some really interesting film school characters and put them in really compelling film school situations, and type them out on paper.

Which we commence doing, with the proviso, announced at our first meeting, that the producer will want pages delivered every Thursday night for review on Friday. Seems fair—sure. We write 20 pages or so the first week and drop them off at the end of work Thursday.

We gather in his office Friday morning. He doesn't throw ashtrays at us or the pages in our face—he also doesn't fire us, but pretty much everything just short of that. He starts with our lack of talent, our unprofessionalism, our sham claim of being writers of anything, ever, the temerity of our taking studio money, and goes on from there. It's a tongue-lashing, a ream-session, it's venomous, sputtering and half-incomprehensible, and it makes Diana and me feel like cockroaches at the bottom of a sink. Then he tells us to rewrite the pages and throws us out.

Somebody with self-respect, anybody nominal, with a personality, even, would walk at this point, realizing they were employed by a mad, sadistic idiot. That never occurred to us. What, and leave show business? Give up the dressing rooms? Brushing shoulders with Gregory Peck? Omar Sharif, for Christ's sake.

So we worked over the pages, gun-shy and blinking, handed them in the next Thursday night, and pretty much backed our way into his office the next morning. This time was worse. Glasses shattered. His secretary stuck her head in. Diana was in tears, and I felt like breathing into a paper bag.

And this became our routine—this was it, the job. We'd write scenes, hand them in, we'd be excoriated, decimated, crucified within an inch of our mental lives on Friday, get a check at the end of the day and go home and cry over the weekend.

We didn't know. We thought this was what screenwriting was like.

And the world conspired to convince us. We were still thrilled to be in Hollywood, old Hollywood, up near Sunset and Vine, and the one part of our day we'd look forward to was searching out someplace for lunch. The old Brown Derby was there, among other places, and walking the streets around Gower was a stroll through the ghosts and spirits of movie history.

One day, walking back to the studio, we saw a crowd on the sidewalk ahead. A city ambulance had pulled up—emergency techs were carrying a withered, parchment-skinned old man on a stretcher from a ratty Moorish apartment. Diana and I pushed through the crowd to see, past the aging extras and toothless cowboys that lived in that part of town. We asked a woman in a muumuu what was going on. She indicated the old guy being carried past us, clearly in the advanced state of something bad, and shook her head. "He used to be one of the top screenwriters in Hollywood," she said.

Twelve weeks of this. Bashing our heads, trying to capture the very souls of film students. Somewhere around the tenth week, Swift's office called us in our dressing rooms and told us to show up for a publicity session. We did—there was a *LA Times* reporter in the office, interviewing him. The production assistants had been called in too—the photographer posed the four of us behind the boss in his chair. Flash. Flash. Back to work.

And then the job was over. I can't claim the script—*Short Ends* it was called, insight into its level of invention—was anything more than 120 pages of stuff. We went home. We waited to hear.

Weeks passed. Then I heard that Swift's boss at the studio had read the script and thrown it in the trash, saying, "Who gives a shit about film students?" I got this from my agent—he was consoling. Diana got the same from hers.

And now the two of us tried to piece it together—what exactly had we just been through? Nothing about the experience made sense—it was arbitrary, wasteful, cruel. Diana and I talked into the night, her in her place, me in my kitchen, like survivors of some disaster who had blacked out for a time during the hurricane or the earthquake and were trying to patch together some kind of continuity. What was the logic of it—why had somebody done that to us?

A few days later, I'm reading the *Times* and there we are, the four of us and him, our producer, a movie-section picture, fuzzy newspaper halftones. The headline is something like, "David Swift Believes in Youth." Below it, close to 100 column inches of pure piffle—how visionary and far-seeing the producer is, how he's not only doing a cutting-edge movie with his finger smack on the zeitgeist, he's ushering four undeserving toads into the Elysium of show business.

"The article," I tell Diana, when I call her. "That's what it was all about. He put us through all that to get his name in the paper."

She's silent. I'm right.

The upside of it? There is one. It was the first screenwriting job I ever had and my worst. I've had bad ones since—who hasn't, big deal—but never one as nasty as the one at Columbia. The best thing to say for it was that it was the first.

# SECRETS OF THE HOLLYWOOD PROS #2:

## Here's How You Get An Agent. Really...

Speak to aspiring writers and the question most frequently asked is, "How do I get an agent?" If you say, "Write something really good," invariably the reply is, "No, really. How do you get an agent?"

Well, Bucko, today is your lucky day. Because fortunately for you, the editor of this book was present at a meeting of the screenwriting faculty at the American Film Institute, where the chair of the program, Leonard Schrader, an Oscar® nominee for his screenplay *Kiss of the Spider Woman*, actually revealed how you can get an agent.

So now—drum roll, please—we reveal for the first time ever in print:

## Leonard Schrader's Guarenteed Twelve-Step Program For Getting An Agent!

## STEP I

Look in *scr(i)pt* or *Creative Screenwriting*, and check the "Spec Sales" page. These give the details of spec script sales, including the names of the agents. See what agents are currently selling a lot of spec scripts.

# STEP 2

Pick out the one who is selling scripts like yours. (If you've written a teen comedy, pick the agent selling teen comedies. That person is the current go-to guy or gal in that genre.)

# STEP 3

Get the agent's phone number. (Hint: Try the phone book, Sparky.)

# STEP 4

Call the agent.

# STEP 5

When the assistant answers, listen carefully to the voice, then hang up.

# STEP 6

Now that you know what the assistant's voice sounds like, wait until 7 p.m., which is when the agent is waiting for a call back from her A-list clients. (Members of the Hollywood A-list know they're on the A-list because, as they're on their way to dinner, the people who work for them are still in their offices waiting for a callback.)

# STEP 7

Call the agent again. If the assistant answers, hang up. Wait 15 minutes and repeat **Step 7** until an unfamiliar voice answers.

# STEP 8

You are now connected to the agent. Calmly call the agent by her first name and introduce yourself by name as a screenwriter who's been reading about all her most recent successes in the trades. Tell her that she is without a doubt the best agent in Hollywood. (Hint: People kiss ass in Hollywood because it works.)

# STEP 9

If you are still connected, the agent respects your balls and savvy for getting this far and is waiting to hear what you want. Tell the agent that you have a spec script that will be another home run for her.

# STEP 10

The silence on the line means that you now have 15 seconds to give the best 15-second pitch she has ever heard.

# STEP 11

If she says, "Send it to me," do it. If the line goes dead, repeat **STEPS 1-10** with another agent.

# STEP 12

If, after four to six weeks, the assistant calls you and says, "[insert your name here], I have [insert agent's name here] on the line for you," enjoy the moment: you now have an agent! If not, repeat **STEPS 1–12**—but this time don't fuck it up: write a really good script before you start looking for an agent!

# BONUS SECRET OF THE HOLLYWOOD PROS #1:

## Choosing A TV Show To Spec

How do you get a job on a television show?

The short answer is by writing an episode of a TV show on "spec," and submitting it to the producers or network executives of a similar show.[2]

But to give you a more substantive answer, I have enlisted the help of Vida Spears, co-creator and executive producer of *Moesha* and co-creator of *The Parkers*. In the mid '80s, when Vida had transitioned from writers' assistant in the production office of *The Jeffersons* to writer, she was part of a workshop for African-American writers sponsored by the Writers Guild. The goal was to prepare black writers for the next step in a television career: story editor. (This was back when "story editor" actually meant "one who edited stories"—that is, supervised other writers, as opposed to its current meaning of "title for junior writers that whizzes by during the end credits.") The workshop was led by the late Helen Levitt, who had begun her career as a writer in the 1950s, as the beard for her black-listed husband, Al. Under the pseudonym of Helen August, she would take meetings with producers (who, for the most part,

---

2. These days, nobody ever gets hired on the same show they've spec'd because it violates the rule that only the staff of a show truly understands its rhythms and nuances—ergo, why the members of the staff are paid the big bucks; thus, ipso facto, your spec script really can't be that good, otherwise, you'd already be a member of the staff. Don't ask, okay? Because it's as arbitrary as my rule that, in order to be taken seriously, all footnotes must contain Latin words or phrases: ipso facto, the three occurrences in this footnote of ipso facto. —Ed.

---

knew exactly who she was, but didn't want their bosses, the studio heads, to know); then, she and Al would write the script. Some of their earliest work aired on Westinghouse Studio One, one of the famed shows from television's "Golden Age." Besides Vida, the group that Helen led included: Vida's partner, Sara Finney, also a future co-creator and exec producer of *Moesha* and *The Parkers*; future Eugene O'Neill Award-winning playwright and screenwriter Kathleen McGhee-Anderson, whose credits include exec-producing *Soul Food* on Showtime; and yours truly, the editor of this book. We learned how to understand the mechanics of a TV show the way you learn how to understand the workings of an M-16 in basic training: we took shows apart and put them back together again until our understanding of how a show works became an autonomous reflex. Everything I know about how to analyze a script and how to study a TV show to understand the way each show is uniquely put together, I owe to Helen (and to the other writers in the group). All of us have done a lot of movin' on up since that workshop, but none of us has ever forgotten Helen Levitt or what she taught us.

Helen's inspiration lives in Vida's insights into writing a spec TV script:

Choosing which show to spec is not a casual decision. Your script will be your representative in the marketplace. And all the attendant clichés—such as, you only get one chance to make a first impression—will apply.

Because, in this case, like attracts like, before picking a show, you must pick your genre. To get an assignment on a comedy, you have to show that you're funny and can tell a 22-minute story with a beginning, middle and end. To show you can write an interpersonal drama, you must reveal your intimate understanding of the workings of the human heart. To demonstrate that you can take an audience through the process of how, like the Mounties, *CSI* always gets their man or woman, you must write what's called a 'police procedural.'

Having picked a genre, choosing which show to spec is like surfing: not only do you need to see the wave before it breaks, you need to see it before anyone else does. Go into any TV series production office and you will see unread stacks of *Frasier* or *Sex And The City* (if the show's a comedy) or *Six Feet Under* or *West Wing* waiting to be recycled. Those were the hot shows to spec several years ago. To be noticed today, you need to spec the show that's going to be hot tomorrow.

Yeah, right. How are you supposed to know that?

You can't. But you can take an educated guess. Pay attention to the buzz in the business. Look for a new show that debuts to both critical plaudits and strong ratings. Why both? Writing the best spec episode of the best show that got canceled after six episodes is a feat akin to predicting the winner of last year's Kentucky Derby.

Once you pick your show, study it. Tape or TiVo episodes. Watch them over and over again. See how they do it. What are the show's arenas? Is it a workplace show or do we go home with the characters? Is it the kind of show where a special guest-star relative shows up and then the hijinks begin? Take out a stopwatch and time how long it takes them to do what they do. How long is each act? Is the timing consistent over several episodes? How much screen time do the secondary characters get? (Hint: If the answer is not much, then don't come up with a story for a secondary character that could be expanded into a three-part special episode for that character because that's not the show they're doing.) If you are in Los Angeles, stop into the Writers Guild Foundation Library where you can read episodes of almost all the shows currently airing.

Which brings me to the point of your analysis. You are trying to discern the voice of the show you're specing. You want your spec episode to compare to the very best work done on that show. And that means that once you get down to writing it, you need to hone and polish it until it glistens like a just-detailed SL500. Remember, your script has gotta represent!

So perhaps the most important advice I can give you is to pick a new show you genuinely like. Write your dream episode of that show. Your passion will make your words come alive.

And maybe your career...

*"You've got to sell your heart..."*

—F. Scott Fitzgerald

# Chapter 3

## INTRODUCTION

## Curveballs:

## Pitching and Selling

Whoever came up with the idea of writers pitching was one of those kids who liked pulling wings off flies. Probably still does.

Think about it. Let's drag a mumble-mouthed, navel-gazing, recalcitrant social retard into an office and make him put on a show! Why would anyone do that, except to take pleasure in the suffering of others?

Yet, this is how most projects in Hollywood begin: A writer with an idea, selling her heart out in the office of someone who's only empowered to say "no." *The Player*—which Carl Gottlieb, the award-winning writer of *Jaws*, is fond of calling the best documentary about Hollywood ever made—got it right. Yet when push comes to shove—or mortgage comes to foreclosure—to survive as a writer in Hollywood, you have to find a way to give them the old razzle-dazzle. (Or if you're pitching a hip-hop project, the new rizzle-dizzle.)[3]

3. Warning: Do not try this at home! By the time you read this, that "izzle" shizzle will be passizzle. Which is how Hip-Hop culture works: if it's made its way into a book, it's no longer hip.—Ed.

I have heard executives say that there is an inverse relationship between a writer's ability to pitch and the writer's ability to write. Many writers I know take comfort in this maxim, even though it may just be what kind-hearted executives say after you've crashed and burned in the room.

In both film and television, the process of pitching is similar. You go into a room and tell someone a story—which is different from telling someone a plot. (The plot is what happens; the story is why anything happens at all.) Take the first *Godfather*. It may take as long to explain its plot as to watch the movie, but its story can be summed up in a single word: family. Not just the family; everyone's family. It looks at family through the lens of one of the most powerful, fundamental myths of the American experience: the immigrant's quest for the American Dream. *The Godfather* is also a meditation on one particular element of family: fathers and sons. It is the story of Michael, the "good" son, and Sonny and Fredo, the sons who disappoint. Its key scene is not one of the archetypical gangster movie moments, such as the assassination of Sonny at the toll booth, but Michael's final moment with his father, in which they discuss who betrayed the family. Vito reveals his now-thwarted dream of Michael one day ascending to the mountaintop of America society: Senator Corleone... Governor Corleone. To which Michael tenderly responds, "We'll get there, Pop." If you were in a room pitching the greatest gangster story ever told, and it all came down to telling the person on the other side of the desk one scene that encapsulates the entire movie, which scene would you pitch—the toll-booth massacre or the father-and-son heart-to-heart?

And perhaps that's the secret to pitching. Our next essayists know that if you have a story that comes from the heart, you can tell it to your shoes and still sell it. Sometimes...

# Andrew W. Marlowe

## The Art of the Pitch

---

*"'Naw...' he said, 'let's just get it over with.'"*

Andrew W. Marlowe's screenwriting credits include *Air Force One, End of Days* and *Hollow Man*. After graduating from USC's School of Cinema-Television in 1992, Marlowe won the Academy of Motion Picture Arts and Sciences' Nicholl Fellowship for emerging screenwriters, for which he received a generous stipend and a beautiful wife.

The girl I'd been living with had decided to go to graduate school back east. For reasons that still elude me, she ended up with custody of our only car, an old Mazda B2000 pickup truck that we bought together when we moved from New York to the West Coast. I used to curse that car because it had no air-conditioning and every time I had a meeting on a warm day, I'd have to bring an extra shirt to change into so I wouldn't look like I'd just stepped out of a sauna. Now that the car was gone, I missed it horribly. Sweaty wheels were much better than no wheels at all. I was just starting out in the business and barely had enough money for rent, let alone another car.

Thankfully, I was on the verge of landing my first writing gig. After months of fruitless pitching on the heels of a coming-of-age

---

spec that didn't sell, I'd finally managed to climb the ladder on a studio project that had some momentum. I'd impressed the creative exec enough to recommend my take to the Vice President of Production. The V.P. couldn't have been nicer. As she sat through my pitch, she smiled and laughed and nodded enthusiastically. It was just the take they were looking for, she said. With warm handshakes all around, I left them to their hushed whispers and retreated home to wait for the follow-up phone call.

"They loved it," my agent said. "Really?" I asked. "Yeah, they want you to go in next week to pitch to the President of Production. It's just a formality though. They really loved your take." I called my parents to tell them the good news and began browsing the classifieds. Not the help wanted ads I usually scanned, but the multi-colored car section.

I'd been borrowing my friends' cars for my meetings, but try as I might, I couldn't scare up a ride for the big day. Luckily the public transportation system in Los Angeles can take you almost anywhere, but the time it takes can vary wildly. Getting from point A to point B might take 40 minutes or it might take four hours. You just have to leave enough time.

I arrived at the studio with an hour and a half to spare. It was way too soon to go in, but there was nothing nearby so I found myself pacing outside the studio walls. Good practice for the next writer's strike, I thought. As I rehearsed the story in my head, I began to imagine the meeting in vivid detail. I would be escorted down the hall to the big man's office where I'd be ushered into the inner sanctum. Mr. Studio President would welcome me warmly and congratulate me on cracking the nut of a very tough story. I would be gracious, witty, and charming, effortlessly tossing off my pitch. We'd have a few laughs, and then he'd shake my hand and say those seven magic words every screenwriter waits to hear,

"We'll have Business Affairs call your agent."

The California sun sat high in the summer sky, and outside the studio walls there was no shelter. I started to sweat worse than Albert Brooks in *Broadcast News*. I hadn't brought an extra shirt because I had no car to leave it in. There must be an air-conditioned building somewhere on the lot where I could hang out for an hour. I headed for the studio entrance.

"There'll be a drive-on for you at the gate," the assistant had said when he called to confirm the meeting. As I approached the entrance, I realized I had a drive-on, but I had nothing to drive on. I looked around for a pedestrian entrance, but didn't see one. Having no idea how to get onto the lot without a car, I fell in line behind the column of vehicles waiting at the security gate. In front of me was a brand new Porsche, behind me a brand new Range Rover. I was trying really hard not to feel like a complete idiot or pass out from exhaust fumes. The only comfort I had was that the meeting was "just a formality". Soon I would be employed. I'd buy a sweet convertible with air-conditioning. Never again would I get caught changing shirts in the studio parking lot by some pretty D-girl. Never again would I humiliate myself by being the only pedestrian in a parade of late-model status cars. When my turn came at the security gate, the guard handed me my pass, cocked his eyebrow and ceremoniously raised the gate arm for me to, uh, walk through.

By the time I got to the air-conditioned Executive Building, I still had 45 minutes to kill. I tried to look purposeful as I studied the movie posters hanging in the hallway, but five may-I-help-yous later, I retreated to the bathroom. I found a quiet stall to hide for the next half-hour, cooling down and composing myself.

I arrived at the V.P.'s office right on time and was ushered in for the requisite small talk while we waited for Mr. Big to call us to his office. Ten minutes later, we ran out of small talk. After an awkward pause, the V.P. apologized for her boss, speculating that a previous meeting must've run late. I assured her it was quite all right and tried to combat the silence by asking about the various trinkets she had in her office. Unfortunately, none of these knickknacks had more than a two-sentence story associated with them. Between brief trinket stories, we waited. And waited. And waited. Nearly an hour later, and nearly five hours after I'd left my apartment that morning, we finally got the nod. Here we go, I thought, and we took the long walk down the hallway to the big man's office.

His assistant was all smiles without a hint of apology as he led us into the wood-paneled, stately inner sanctum. But the chair behind the desk was empty. Where was Mr. Big? I heard moaning coming from behind me. I turned around to find the Studio President lying on his couch writhing in pain. "Oh my God. Are you all right?" some idiot asked. It was a pretty stupid question given the circumstance, and I was instantly sorry that I was the idiot who asked it.

"Does it look like I'm all right? I just threw my goddamn back out and my fucking chiropractor can't see me for another hour!" He finally looked up and saw me for the first time. "Who the fuck are you?" he growled. My good friend, the V.P., seemed genuinely thrown and completely unsure of how to proceed. I jumped in.

"I'm the writer. But look, I'm sure the last thing you want to do is listen to my pitch while you're lying there in pain. Let's reschedule." Formality or no, this was clearly not the moment.

He looked me up and down, and then he uttered those seven magic words I never in my life expected to hear.

"Naw…" he said, "let's just get it over with."

I didn't get the job.

# Ken Nolan

## On Not Pitching

---

*"I discovered (to my dawning horror) that after you sell your spec script, you have to go in and explain it to them."*

Ken Nolan has sold several spec scripts, none of which were ever made into actual movies. But he did write the screenplay for *Black Hawk Down*, which won him a Writers Guild Award nomination in 2002. He is currently working on a Warner Bros. project called *The Forge of God*, which he hopes will be made into a very expensive film.

I suffer from pitch-o-phobia, or "P.O.P." as it is described in the *New England Journal of Medicine*. The thought of "POPing" makes me break into a cold sweat. Walking into an executive's office and "weaving a story" or "captivating my audience through spoken words" makes my heart palpitate with dread. Just writing about it at this moment is making me jittery. And so, like the driver who is afraid of driving on the freeways, I have learned to take a complex network of side streets to arrive at my destination.

When I think back on the evasion and elusion tactics I've employed over the last ten years to avoid pitching, it makes me shake my head with wonder. Such energy expended to avoid the pitch! If there was a Marvel Comics Superhero who avoided pitching, he'd be drawn in my image. His powers would be procrastination and pitch avoidance. A double threat. He'd be called "The Evasive Evader." Or "The Wondrous Avoider." (Note: consider "The Deflector." It's simple and I think people would find it less difficult to say than the previous possible names. Let's discuss at next meeting.)

You see, the reason I became a writer was to *write*. My strength is in writing, not in telling a story out loud. I didn't take the "Telling Your Story Out Loud" class at college. I took writing classes.

At the start of my "career," I stuck mostly to writing spec scripts. There was no one calling me up during the writing process, hassling me about the pitch I'd sold them, wanting to add their creative two cents: "We just want to be in on the fun, Ken! Can we go over that first act again? How about if I just run through it, then you repeat it back to me, throwing in whatever new stuff you want as we go? It's a free-form thing here. No idea is too crazy! Ready? Wait, I got a better idea, Ken. Why don't you start, then I'll repeat it back to you. Okay? Go for it, buddy! Let it sing! Let it flow!"

Not only could I not pitch, but also the plots of my spec scripts were never really "pitchable" anyway. Some ideas are like that. Try to pitch *Field of Dreams*. Imagine sitting in front of a room full of grim-faced studio executives and weaving your story: "A guy in Iowa realizes he needs to put a baseball field out in his cornfield, but he doesn't have the money to really lose the crops, but he does it anyway. The reason he does this is because a voice in the corn, uh… in the cornfield, uh, tells him to do it. And… and so, uh, so he DOES IT! Isn't that great? Yeah, so he makes a baseball field, but, but he also kidnaps James Earl Jones. Wait, that's too far ahead. But his brother-in-law is gonna repossess his cornfield. Crap, I'm doing it wrong. Did I mention Ray Liotta's character yet? Shoeless Joe? Oh, he's great, he's really intense. He comes out of the cornfield one night. He's a ghost... Uh, is it hot in here? Do you have an air-conditioning unit? Can I sit in front of it? Can I hug it? Mommy!"

When my friends used to ask me, "What are you working on?," I'd try to pitch them the spec I was writing, and as I spoke, I'd watch as their eyes slowly and inevitably glazed over. They might say something like, "... Huh," as I finished "weaving my tale." Or they might utter something like "Sounds... good..." I don't even bother trying to pitch to my friends anymore, that's how bad I am at pitching. Anyway, I sold those damned spec scripts, so there. Who's laughing now? HUH? THE *DEFLECTOR*, that's who!

This may sound naïve, but I never knew when I became a screenwriter that I'd have to *talk*. In fact, Studio Executives seem to want you to talk all the time. Writing makes up about 10 percent of what I do. The other 90 percent is talking, returning calls, reading, going to meetings, playing unhealthy amounts of X-Box, talking, talking, meeting, talking. *Talking!* For God's sake!

All this time, I thought I was going to be able to avoid pitching. Instead I've been constantly forced to do mini-pitches. Mini-pitches are where the Execs and I have to talk out the third act, or I have to go in to the head of the studio and tell him or her what the focus of the next rewrite will be. Mini-pitches involve talking. And pitching. Lots of it. Mini-pitches, like land mines in some far-off war-torn country, are everywhere. Sometimes you don't even know you're in a mini-pitch until you've stepped on one, and then you're plastered against some wall in someone's office, watching your guts seep out as you hem and haw and desperately try to sound intelligent.

Unfortunately, I don't think the mini-pitch can be avoided. They just sneak up on you, clever little devils that they are. But the big pitch *can* be avoided. You can take the side streets and the back streets of pitching and stay off the freeway, if you really want to work hard.

So, what are the side streets? How can you too avoid this pitch thing? Well, you can write a spec script. Write a spec script and you don't have to go in and pitch. Right? Wrong. Dead wrong.

I discovered (to my dawning horror) that after you sell your spec script, you have to go in and *explain* it to them. You have to justify what you've written: "Why does your main character do that? Why does he do this? What's his arc? Where's he going? What does he want? Is there a motivating force behind his actions? Why isn't he more heroic? What does the ending mean?"

Another solution: find a book to adapt, get the rights yourself, and start adapting it on your own. You can even write a treatment for this, which forces executives to read. Two years ago, I wrote a 75-page treatment outlining my concept for a book adaptation and sold the whole idea to Warner Bros. A 70-plus page treatment, you say? Madness. Why would I do that? Doesn't that seem a bit insane? To be honest, it was mostly to avoid the pitch.

When I auditioned to be hired to adapt *Black Hawk Down* for Jerry Bruckheimer, I was terrified that I'd have to come in and pitch my "take" to Jerry. So I came clean with the execs and said, "Look, I really want to write this project, but I think if I have to go in and explain it to your boss, it would be a recipe for disaster. I'll be so nervous I won't be able to talk. I can't keep all the thoughts and threads in my head." They looked at me, faces registering slight befuddlement, and asked if I would perhaps like to write a treatment instead. "A treatment? Why, yes!" No pitching! Of course, a treatment involved more work than a pitch, and I ended up writing three 50-page, single-spaced treatments before I got to go to the script phase, but I think it was worth it in the long run. And honestly, it probably kept me employed longer. A treatment is malleable. A script is so concrete. You screw up on a treatment and you write it again. You screw up on a script and you may be fired.

Pitching just wasn't in the cards for me. I tried it once and I ended up having a panic attack and turning bright red, and having more sweat pour down my face than Shaq in game seven of the NBA Championship. That was the end of my pitching career.

Don't get me wrong. Those who can pitch well should do so at all costs. I applaud them for their savvy gift of storytelling. I do not possess their talent. I tip my hat to them and bid them bon voyage. But with a parting warning, spoken in a whisper, like the Ancient Mariner clutching their forearm, hissing at them: "If you pitch it, you eventually have to write it."

# Sandra Tsing Loh

## Punching Up the Chicken

---

*"...that's my advice to young writers: 'Write TO the beak flaps.'"*

When she's not punching up scripts, Sandra Tsing Loh is a writer/performer whose commentary series, *The Loh Life* (KPCC) and *The Loh Down* (Marketplace), can be heard on public radio. Her books include *Depth Takes A Holiday, A Year in Van Nuys, Aliens In America* and the novel *If You Lived Here, You'd Be Home By Now*. She's also a contributing editor to *The Atlantic Monthly*, which requires quite a BIT of punch up.

I have one of the best Hollywood gigs ever. My friend Julia Sweeney once used the phrase "trophy writer," aka: a writer whose mere presence on a project adds excitement, whether or not they end up doing much—if any—of the heavy lifting. Actually, I think of myself as less "trophy writer" than a kind of a "Heisman trophy writer." I myself am vague about sports and sports awards. Which I think is much like the vagueness people feel about me. Mostly known from public radio, mine is an underground cult status, which means while standing at the Sherman Oaks Trader

Joe's, the person ahead may whip around confusedly at the sound of my VOICE.

As a Heisman Trophy Writer (and, yes, our employment IS somewhat occasional), I don't get called for the big stuff, aka: third act in collapse, star in rehab, director needs to be pitched some brilliant new *Memoirs of a Geisha*-style literary approach Scott Rudin's suggesting about... Wha—? No, I get little jewels of jobs, quick little mini-tartlets, like the call to "punch up"... *Chicken Little!*

Know that on animated features, the GROUP punch-up can be grisly, the comedy round-table an actual vision of hell. There you are, locked in a room with ten white male comedy writers named Josh. When the movie rolls, you all start yelling funny things at the screen. The awkwardness comes when you yell a line at the same time as the guy sitting to your right, Josh Number #7. It seems The Room is laughing at his line rather than yours—but perhaps it's simply because Oh Room O' Joshes didn't hear it, so in the ensuing silence, you forge boldly ahead and yell again, somewhat more loudly: "So I'm sayin'... BOO-yaa!" Whose humor—such as it was—was really all... in the... timing. And why are you suddenly sounding, in the silence, like a gay Jimmie JJ Walker? You're a freak! For today, a very well-paid freak, but a freak nonetheless.

By contrast, the *Chicken Little* job was the much more preferable Greta Garbo-like SOLO punch-up, at the Disney Aladdin Hat building (I call it the "D.A.H.") in Burbank. You swoosh past classic Snow White cels to your own office, semiprivate cappuccino machine, personal rad Marshall stack of video and DVD players. Unlike the rest of Hollywood—particularly in the ALARMINGLY FRESH, HIP WORLD OF NETWORK SITCOMS!—most of the inhabitants of D.A.H. are poorly dressed, Bozo the Clown haired, and generally have the fallen air of melancholy Hobbits.

They've been padding through the twilit corridors of D.A.H. for 20 years because no other living human beings understand Animation. "I'm f&**ing hot!" you suddenly think, making a kind of "rock on!" fist. Understand that I am 43 years old and weigh 144 pounds on a very good day. So my job is to "hip up" the Chicken. Everyone working on the film is BRILLIANT, but the film has been, now, what… five, seven, ten years on the making. In that time the Chicken has changed sexes; characters have been killed; there's a board upon which are posted—in that Great Circle of Life—photos of actual cast and crew babies born. The Chicken, as the script suggests, is white meat. He's now voiced by Zach Braff, who sounds Yiddish… while singing Queen. Which means the major cultural influence we're missing is hip-hop! Boo-yaa! Sitting alone in my office, I excitedly concoct strange "Island of Dr. Moreau meets MC Hammer" bird-flu type experiments. Instead of "That girl is cute," I might try: "That chick is BIRDYLICIOUS!"

My bosses Mark Dindal and Randy Fulmer are welcoming— they encourage creative flow. But the reality is, while rewriting is cheap, reanimation's expensive. It reminds me of an IMAX movie rewrite I did for McGillivray-Freeman (*Everest*) where I'd pen in thrilling directions like: "SMASHCUT TO ISLAND OF BORA BORA!" And Greg McGillivray (a Scotsman) would say, somewhat wryly, "If I could even find a cameraman who could physically do what you're describing, that shot would cost me 2 million dollars." So I took Dindal and Fulmer's advice to write as the beak was already flapping—that's my advice to young writers: "Write TO the beak flaps." Dialogue went in, there were hugs all around, Chicken Little lunchboxes for my kids.

And here I sit awaiting my next delicately-nuanced comedy punch-up job, hockey stick in stand.

# SECRETS OF THE HOLLYWOOD PROS #3:

## Pitch Your Cat

In Hollywood, you can beat death and taxes. Think about it: what writer is hotter than Shakespeare and further out of the reach of the IRS? But sooner or later, everybody has to pitch. And if you're going to survive, you have to find a way to do it well.

Like getting to Carnegie Hall, the secret of a great pitch is practice, practice, practice. At a recent Writers on Genre conference sponsored by the Writers Guild Foundation, Michael Miner, co-author of *Robocop*, advised writers to hone their pitches by pitching to anyone who'll listen. If need be, "tell it to your cat."

The brilliance of this idea is staggering because cats are very much like many executives (and agents): self-absorbed creatures with short attention spans and sushi breath. Moreover, pitching to a cat requires the same delicate balance that must be maintained when pitching to an executive (or agent): if you're uninteresting, the cat's eyes will glaze over and it will either leave, fall asleep or start licking itself—which is the human equivalent of leaving, falling asleep or taking a cell phone call. Get hyper, not only will the cat become skittish and try everything in its power not to be in the same room with you now or ever again, but the memory of your insanity will pervade the collective cat unconscious, and other cats will avoid you like a cold fleabath.

How do you structure a good pitch?

Ron Bass says the inspiration for *My Best Friend's Wedding* was the notion of doing a Julia Roberts movie in which Julia Roberts doesn't get the guy. Sounds like a great opening line to me. This strategy of announcing a clever summary of the story—in this case, one that goes against type in a provocative way—can be especially effective in pitching episodes of TV shows, where the characters and their universe are a given (and essentially not malleable) and the goal of the pitch is to repurpose the familiar in a surprising and satisfying way.

Another effective way to start a pitch is with an epiphany: a Raymond Chandler two-guys-come-through-the-door-with-guns-aimed-at-your-hero moment from your movie. This is starting the pitch on the central dramatic question. For example, a kindly waitress lets an obviously mentally unbalanced man in out of the rain. The man sits at the piano and plays like a virtuoso. Who is he—and how did he wind up here? He would be pianist David Helfgott and this would be a great way to begin to pitch *Shine*. (And was also a great way to open the movie.) Beginning with a bang forces you to quickly get to the point: who's your protagonist, how did she get in this jam, and, most importantly, how is she going to get out? Remember, cats like to toy with things that move.

Wherever you start your pitch, you end up in the same ballpark: trying to tell a compelling story about a character with a problem who makes a choice. That's the essence of drama. If you can make the audience feel something, that's great drama. If you're pitching a comedy, then you have to tell a funny story about a funny character with a funny problem that becomes really funny because the funny character makes a really funny choice. If the audience laughs, that's comedy. If they laugh a lot, that's a miracle. As the punch line to the old show biz joke goes: dying is easy; comedy is hard.

Knowing what to pitch, however, is pretty simple. To paraphrase Sarah Lutz, co-author of *Legally Blonde*, don't pitch the movie you think the studio wants to buy; pitch the movie you want to see. Put it this way, if they knew what they wanted, they wouldn't be asking you to tell them what it is.

But above all, when you pitch, remember who you're pitching to. If your pitch is just the externalization of your ordeal of pitching, it's gonna be nappy time or "exit, stage right"; but if it's a nice fat mouse, the cat may just pounce.

*"Lindsay goes round the table and introduces everyone—making it clear that I am present in the capacity of 'writer' rather than actress, therefore no one has to be nice to me."*

— Emma Thompson, from
*The Sense & Sensibility Screenplay & Diaries*

# Chapter 4

## INTRODUCTION

## Visions and Revisions:

## The Script Monster

To paraphrase Cervantes, every good movie or TV show is a happy accident.

And—to keep the allusion to great novelists going—every bad movie, like an unhappy marriage, is bad in its own way.

With each *FADE IN:*, every screenwriter seeks to write something great.

Personally, each time I see *FADE OUT* approaching in a first draft, I begin readying my Academy Award® or Emmy® Award acceptance speech. Then, I read the draft and get depressed when I realize how far short I've fallen of what I had hoped to achieve. After a few days of lying motionless in bed with my head under the covers—which my cats enjoy, but my wife and children don't—I get my ass in gear and do the work that needs to be done.

But the agony of getting it right on the page is by no means a guarantee of experiencing the ecstasy of seeing your words on the stage. In fact, it's no guarantee that the ecstasy will be, in fact, ecstasy.

The greatest moment in a writer's life is undoubtedly the first time you look up at a movie screen, heart swelling as you want to jump out of your seat and scream to the crowd, "I wrote that!" But the worst may well be, just as undoubtedly, the moment you look up at the screen as you slump in your seat, heart sinking, as you realize, "I wrote that?"

Writers have an often uneasy relationship with the process of filmmaking. Many of us believe that screenplays are the literature of the Media Age. All of us must accept—like it or not—that a screenplay is also the blueprint for a movie that will be realized through the work of other artists. In television, writers literally run the show. But the grind of turning out two-dozen television episodes in 40 weeks is such that, even on a critically acclaimed show such as *The West Wing*, its creator Aaron Sorkin noted at the last Words into Pictures conference that the showrunner knows that a half-dozen episodes will be great, a half-dozen will be dogs—and the rest, you just try to get through.

In our next essay, Chris Abbott philosophically notes that "the agony is the ecstasy." And so she begins our next essays: tales of happy accidents, just getting through it—and surviving lions and tigers and *bolas?!* Oh, my!

# Chris Abbott

## The Agony Is The Ecstasy

*"It can be as good as you're willing to make it."*

Chris Abbott, whose credits include *Little House on the Prairie, Magnum, P.I.* and *Dr. Quinn, Medicine Woman*, has been writing and producing network television drama for 20 years. She is currently trying to decide what to do with the next 20 years.

Several years ago, I was living in Richmond, Virginia, shooting a series I had created for UPN called *Legacy*. Like any new series, we had experienced our share of birthing pains. Right out of the chute, we found ourselves prepping a two-hour episode from an outline while we completely rewrote the script. The director, who had every reason to be unhappy with this plan of action, had shown remarkable patience. But by the last day of shooting, tempers had grown short and I was called to the set to keep the director and the cinematographer from coming to blows.

Producing an episode of television is a bit like building a skyscraper. Only in television, you often have to hire the architect, the contractor, the laborers, the interior decorator, the management team, the secretaries, the assistants, the executive dining room chef and the janitor all at the same time—all before you have even a floor plan on paper. They, in turn, have to submit budgets based on what they think the cost of steel might be, or how many people will be eating in the dining room, and those budgets have to be approved by an executive sitting in an office far, far away before the actual construction can begin.

Under these conditions, it's no wonder so little good television gets made. The wonder is that so much good television gets made.

I came to Hollywood, like many people, to become a movie star. After several years of spectacular failure in that arena, it occurred to me that I ought to try something else. Maybe something like writing. The fact that I had never studied writing didn't worry me. I had certainly read a lot of books and seen a lot of movies.

Getting hired to write in Hollywood depends not on how well you can write but on how well you can talk. The pitch meeting resembles what the prehistoric campfire story-telling ritual must have looked like: people sitting in a semicircle with one wild-eyed story teller in front, painting visual pictures for the others.

My first pitch was an unnerving event. I had worked out a light-hearted comedy: boy meets girl, boy loses girl, boy gets girl and then realizes, too late, that wasn't what he wanted after all. My agent had booked a meeting for me to pitch this story to the Vice President of American International Pictures, the "B-Studio" megalith originally founded by Samuel Z. Arkoff.

The gold-chain-wearing studio Vice President waved me into his office when I knocked on his door and then kept me waiting over 20 minutes, taking one call after another, each of which seemed to pertain to his travel plans or his sexual prowess or both. I was impressed. I couldn't have talked on either subject for more than five minutes, ten at the most. He didn't bother taking his feet off the desk before he addressed me. "I read your script," he said.

"I didn't like it."

"What am I doing here?" I thought.

"Your agent tells me you have something better."

"It's dawn in New York City," I said. "Steam rises from the manhole covers as we tilt up to see—"

"What?" he said.

"My story. It's set in New York City."

I stuttered out a few more sentences, detailing the characters. He interrupted me again.

"You call this a story?" he said.

The question seemed to require an answer.

"Yes," I said.

"I don't call this a story. I call this a fuckin' TV show. Who are these fuckin' characters? You expect me to care about these people? I don't give a rat's ass about these people. You're fuckin' wasting my valuable time."

I called my agent after I left his office.

"He didn't like the story," she told me.

"I got that," I said.

Within a year, I had sold a script to Michael Landon. A few short months later, he hired me as a story editor for *Little House on the Prairie* and two years later, I was living in Hawaii, writing for the CBS series *Magnum, P.I.* starring Tom Selleck.

In the middle of our last season, we had run out of material. I had to write a complete script over the weekend. I went into a full-blown panic. I decided to do a relaxation meditation just to calm down enough to begin. In my meditation, I came across John Huston. He was sitting on a boulder overlooking the ocean.

"I'll write it for you," he said.

I stood there, looking at him.

"Just go back to the typewriter and type. It'll be fine."

Writing so fast it seemed I was reading it rather than writing it, I completed the script by Monday. The script was enthusiastically received and we began prep on time.

Between *Magnum* and *Legacy*, I wrote for ten different series on four different networks. I don't know how anyone survives the pace of writing for television. It's like hopping a freight train at 50 miles an hour. But it's only scary if you think about it first. Writing fast, writing collaboratively, writing genre (or as some would say, "formula") is challenging, no question about it. But like every other kind of writing, it can be as good as you're willing to make it.

# Billy Riback

## Too Many Words

*"'My problem is,' she said, 'there are too many words on the page.'"*

Billy Riback's credits include episodes of *Murphy Brown, Grown Ups, Carol & Company* and 14 scripts for *Home Improvement*, which he also produced during its first five seasons. His debits include his car and his apartment.

I remember the day all too well... like a first kiss, or a first bike ride, or, in this case, more like the first time you step on a rusty nail. I had been walking around Venice Beach that glorious, summer Sunday afternoon, but the phone call was coming to my house at three. Back in those days, I didn't have a cell, so I had to get home on time. It was only years later that I discovered that even if you do have a Nokia 1290-A17, trying to talk on it from Venice Beach is like trying to have a normal conversation during a Passover Seder.

So I raced home, although I admit I did stop off at Foster's for a banana milkshake. It was spectacular, but the initial brain freeze I got from that first sip was surely a harbinger of things to come. As I entered my apartment at precisely three o'clock, the phone was already ringing. I was nervous and excited—the studio was calling me with their reaction to my pilot script. They had to love it, I thought. Nobody in Los Angeles makes a business call on the weekend, on time, to deliver bad news. Eagerly, I picked up the phone.

"Hey, Billy," the voice said.

"Hey, Keith," (not her real name) I said. Then there was a hideous, long pause. What was she holding back? I hoped she was having a heart attack. When someone's calling you, aren't they supposed to initiate the conversation? Already, I regretted picking up the phone. Reluctantly, I plunged in.

"So, what did you think?" Another long pause. I felt like suggesting to her that this might be easier with a series of dots and dashes. However, the odds of this executive learning Morse code were long, longer than the odds of rap music being played at Strom Thurmond's funeral.

Finally, after what seemed like an eternity, she spoke. "I read your script."

Good start, I thought. At least she didn't eat it. "And?" I inquired.

"I liked it." That took long enough. Why was this like pulling teeth? Couldn't we have a normal conversation? You know the kind... she talks, I talk, she talks, I talk, then one of us says they have to go. This wasn't that type of conversation. This is how they should torture people who call you during dinner, mispronounce your name, and tell you you've been specially selected to win a free trip to Guatemala to look at condos.

"So you liked it?" I said. "Any notes?"

"A few," she responded. I settled in for the day.

"What have you got?" I boldly asked.

"Well," she said, "the thing is, I've got a big problem with the act break."

Let me take a moment here. The studio and I had agreed on exactly what the act break should be. Basically, she was about to criticize the studio. Why didn't she make the studio come home early from Venice Beach? With as little attitude as I could muster, which I can guarantee was a ton of attitude, I asked what the problem was. Let me preface her response with a little explanation. The act break was a one-page montage, neatly spaced, in which our lead character tried on a series of disguises.

Any writers who are reading this should now step away from all open windows.

"My problem is," she said, "there are too many words on the page." Remember that brain freeze I got at Foster's? Nothing compared to this moment.

Incredulous, I asked her what she meant. "Just what I said," she answered haughtily. "I can't read that many words." At that point I thought, *War and Peace*, probably not on her bookshelf.

"I'm a writer," I fought back. "I can't write without words. You wouldn't tell I.M. Pei, 'too many bricks.'"

"Who?" she said. I knew going in that making that analogy was a huge mistake.

"Look," I pleaded, addressing her as if she were starring in an all-female version of *Cuckoo's Nest*, "it's just one page. How hard can it be to read one page?"

"I don't have the time," she said. "And I know the woman at the network has the same problem."

I remember thinking that she and the network honchoette had way bigger problems than that. I wasn't sure if ignorance and stupidity were the types of problems that could be solved by therapy, but they certainly could be solved by an assassin's bullet.

"Maybe I could White-Out every other word," I suggested.

"Are you being sarcastic?" she inquired.

"I don't know. Is sarcastic too many syllables?"

"Look," she finally snapped. "You have no choice. There has to be more space on the page." Obviously that was so she would have some place to color.

"Just out of curiosity," I said. "Did you actually read the page or did you stop when you saw this avalanche of letters?"

"I couldn't get through it."

"So you don't even know the content," I said, amazed.

"No," she said. "The content doesn't matter if there's too many words in the content."

We're talking about one page, ladies and gentlemen. This is like not being able to finish alphabet soup because there are too many letters in the bowl.

Reluctantly, I caved. What was I supposed to do? I knew that we were going to lose this critical montage, not because it wasn't funny, but because I was dealing with someone who had the attention span of bubble wrap. Taking out words meant undermining the show's premise—and losing six or seven certain laughs in the process. But, clearly, I had no choice.

"How about this?" I offered. "Let's just take out the whole page."

"That would make me very happy," she responded. "Have a

great weekend."

"You, too," I lied, and hung up. I momentarily contemplated becoming a manicurist.

I guess the moral is simple. Studio executives are vastly overpaid, for the sole purpose of annoying people who painstakingly string thoughts together to hopefully entertain and occasionally enlighten. If I were to edit their contracts, I'd have one response: "Too many zeroes."

By the way, the pilot was picked up and did make it onto the fall schedule. But, we were soon canceled, for the one thing worse than too many words... not enough viewers.

# Steve Shagan

## You Gotta Shoot Something

---

*"Mort, with all due respect, there are no tigers in Africa.'"*

Steve Shagan has been nominated for Academy Awards® for his screenplays of *Voyage of the Damned* and *Save the Tiger*, which also won the Writers Guild Award as best original screen drama. He is *The New York Times* best-selling author of *The Formula* and *Pillars of Fire*. His most recent film credits are *Primal Fear* and, for HBO, *The John Gotti Story*, which earned him an Emmy®.

Many moons ago, Sy Weintraub, the owner of the *Tarzan* television series filming in Mexico for NBC, hired me to replace the fourth producer of the troubled series. My credentials were impeccable. I had never before produced anything, but I spoke Spanish, had no agent, needed the gig, and still considered *Tarzan* to be one of my film heroes; a man who loved animals and was suspect of humans.

In late February, I arrived on the set in a dense jungle north of Acapulco. No matter how hard the crew worked to clear a space, the jungle belonged to reptiles, insects and a strain of fierce ants. Night shooting was out of the question. Within minutes of being struck, an arc light would be covered by a wide variety of winged creatures. The constant change of producers and story editors had created a shortage of scripts. We were only ten days from our Friday 7pm airdate. All of this combined with Montezuma's enduring revenge created a state of constant surreal anxiety. We began to feel haunted by past Tarzans. Reflecting back on those maddening times, I can safely say that the entire enterprise was saved by the efforts of a superb Mexican crew and by the gifted Jackson Gillis, a writer who could spit story. He somehow kept the pages coming.

Despite constant problems, we managed to press on, barely making our airdates, using an inordinate amount of old Tarzan stock footage and repeating the same action gags. Mysteriously, the Nielsens began to climb and I had become accustomed to the pervading frantic atmosphere, but nothing prepared me for the unique calamity waiting in the wings.

One afternoon, in my tent at the jungle location, I was rewriting a sequence that for one reason or another we couldn't shoot. It was almost noon. I poured a shot of tequila, drank it straight (ice was dangerous). Montezuma was ever present. At that moment, the revered and imposing Mexican production manager, Don Alfonso Sanchez Tello, entered the tent.

"Buenos dias, Don Alfonso," I greeted him.

"We're in trouble, Señor. Tarzan cannot fight the lion in next week's segment. We cannot proceed."

"What's the problem?"

"It's Major, his *bolas* are the size of melons. A wheelbarrow is supporting them. Dr. Moreno believes a bug of some kind has infected him."

I should explain that "bolas" is Mexican slang for testicles. Major was a harmless, docile pussycat, a great movie lion. We all loved him.

"Is Major in pain?" I asked.

"Dr. Moreno has given him a shot of morphine." Alfonso explained. "He's taken blood and running tests."

"Don't we have a back-up lioness?"

"Yes, Leona, but she despises Tarzan. She growls when she senses his presence. The trainer says it would be too dangerous to use her."

"Why do we have her?"

Alfonso shrugged, "She keeps Major happy, Señor."

In those days, direct dialing from Mexico was a distant fantasy. It took two hours before I finally tracked Sy Weintraub to his partner's tennis court in Beverly Hills. Sy was annoyed with my intrusive call and simply refused to discuss Major's situation.

"I resent this call," he said, "you're the producer—produce! Get that goddamn bohunk to fight Leona!"

"Too dangerous, Sy," I said, feeling the tequila beginning to heat up. "Female lions are unpredictable."

"Then why is she on the payroll?" he asked.

"Maybe they ran out of Christians in Mexico."

"I don't find that amusing. Get ahold of yourself. Use the giant-clam gambit."

"We used it last week."

"Well, Tarzan can bolt into stock footage."

"My predecessors used it to death."

"Then burn the fucking village. You've gotta shoot something. I have my hands full. I'm negotiating the acquisition of a Gauguin painting." He then hung up.

"We're in trouble, Alfonso." I sighed and redialed the international operator.

I placed a call to Mort Werner, head of programming at NBC in New York. While waiting, I thought of what a marvelous cut this would be in a film—from this steaming jungle to snowflakes dancing around Werner's glass-wrapped office.

"What's up, kid?" Mort's voice was warm and friendly. I explained the problem in clinical detail. There was a long pause, "Have you considered tying up Major's testicles and shooting around them?"

"Mort, you have to understand. Major is in one cage and his testicles are in another supported by a wheelbarrow. Besides, he's sedated with morphine. Shooting around his *bolas* is not an option!"

"His what?"

"Balls—balls, Mort."

"Well, what other animals do you have?"

I went down the list. After rejecting the panther, the leopard, the python and the crocodile, he dejectedly asked, "Is there anything else?"

"We do have a young tiger, but we can't use him."

"Why not? The tiger's perfect!"

"Mort, with all due respect, there are no tigers in Africa."

"No one knows that," he replied.

"Come on, Mort, we play to millions of kids, school teachers, zoologists, anthropologists—we'll be inundated with protests. We'll be raw meat for comics and cartoonists."

"Listen to me, Steve," his voice assumed a hard edge, "we could run black leader and get a rating. Never overestimate the intelligence of the television audience. I guarantee that we will not receive a single complaint. Have Tarzan fight the tiger. Hell, we're in a jam. We have to take some license. You gotta shoot something. Take care, kid. Regards to Sy."

Tarzan fought the tiger and for the first time, the show dominated its time slot.

Mort Werner was right. Neither NBC nor Sy's Banner Productions received one letter, telex, telegram or phone call in protest. In one fell swoop we had altered the historic anthology of the African continent. There was now a tiger in Africa by way of Mexico.

Finally, with careful and tender treatment, Major's testicles were cured and he returned triumphantly to the company and his beloved companion, Leona.

The fact that we had deceived the audience bothered me for a while (about ten minutes). After all, when your *bolas* are on the line, you gotta shoot something.

# Alan Kirschenbaum

## One Joke

---

*"If we do this right, this joke could get us on the air."*

Alan Kirschenbaum has written, produced, and directed episodes of *Yes, Dear, Everybody Loves Raymond, Coach, Down the Shore, Anything But Love* and *Dear John.* He continues to work in television to support his actual career of breeding, raising and racing harness racehorses. God help him.

Sometimes, it all comes down to one joke. Or one line, or one moment, or even one image, I guess, but in comedy, it's one simple, beautiful, perfect joke. The series *Yes, Dear*, which I created with my partner Greg Garcia, would never have gotten on the air without a sight gag near the very end of the pilot script, a gag that I'm very lucky to say my partner came up with, a gag that is directly responsible for over a hundred people making comfortable livings for the past three seasons.

The *Yes, Dear* pilot told a story in which Greg Warner, our hero, was assigned the task of caring for his young son Sammy while his wife, Kim, was off to a spa with her recently-moved-in sister, Christine. Christine's husband, Jimmy, and their two young boys were also at home with Greg and Sam. Jimmy was, and continues to be, a bad influence on Greg, and in this case convinced him that rather than spend the day at the hot playground with the kids, as they have told their wives they would, they should instead go to an Indian casino and gamble. Against his better judgment, Greg agrees.

While at the casino, Sammy takes his first shaky steps and walks for the first time. Greg joyfully videotapes the momentous occasion, but then realizes he cannot show Kim the tape or he will be caught in his lie. To the rescue rides Jimmy, who takes the tape to a friend of his who is an editor and has the background changed from the casino to a park. When Greg shows the tape to Kim, Sammy appears to take his first steps in a bucolic Los Angeles park, and Greg is elated, until Sammy starts to walk across a beautiful, shimmering lake.

It seemed funny in the stage directions, but it wasn't until we actually saw the footage the day we were shooting the pilot that we realized just how funny the gag was. So I was very careful to give explicit instructions to the audience switcher, who provides the feed to the live audience, how to cut the footage against the reactions of the characters. Somehow, instinctively, I knew the stakes, and I told her, "If we do this right, this joke could get us on the air."

When it played in front of the live audience, it was like an explosion—loud and long and rolling. Greg and I looked at each other; between us, we'd produced hundreds of sitcom episodes and we'd never heard a laugh like that. When we submitted the rough cut to the network, we were told that Leslie Moonves, the head of CBS, was laughing so hard he was banging his hand on his desk. When they showed it to the focus group at the network testing session, the needle actually pinned at the highest mark, something the testing people said they had never seen before. And, finally, when CBS introduced the fall lineup that May at Carnegie Hall, that clip was shown and a jaded audience of advertising people laughed just as loud and just as long.

The pilot for *Yes, Dear* was a good, solid, professional episode of a series with great potential, which made it better than most. But quickly, people who had no idea what *Yes, Dear* was started talking about "that one where the kid walks on water." There were plenty of other pilots that spring that had potential, but most of them never got a chance to be in the race, a chance to reach that potential. Because they didn't have that one great joke. And sometimes, that's all it takes.

# Jim Kouf

## The One That Got Away

*"I thought to myself, is he accusing me of not stealing Shakespeare?"*

Jim Kouf is a screenwriter who has a lot of credits, including *Stakeout, Rush Hour* and *National Treasure*—and is still wondering when it's going to get easier.

At this point in my screenwriting career, after several films have been made, I have come to the conclusion that it is a miracle any film ever comes out good. Just good mind you. Not great. For a film to come out great would require something greater than a miracle. I don't know what that is, except maybe stupid, blind, dumb-ass luck. But as disheartening as it is to have one of your babies go bad despite all that hard work and best intentions, it's even more disheartening to have actually seen one that could have been a contender wind up flat on its face, especially if it happens because of something completely out of your control. That something is, and I shudder as I mention it, the test screening.

You see, I did this picture called *Stakeout* and it was pretty successful. So, as it happens in Hollywood, when you have a successful picture, you get the opportunity to make another one. This opportunity was *Another Stakeout*. And I wrote a pretty tight screenplay that had a nice dramatic structure, just like the first *Stakeout*. And it had a lot of comedy in it, just like the first *Stakeout*. But, the people I did *Another Stakeout* with, who were the same people I did the first one with, decided—at some point foreign to me—that we had a nice comedic structure with a lot of drama in it. Now, that may not sound like a bad thing until people hit the floor and start trying to get laughs where no laughs were really meant to be. There is nothing wrong with laughs. I love laughs. But I have learned that one should not try too hard to get them because what you're trying to do begins to seem like what you're trying to do and then what you're trying to do makes people realize that they're being manipulated and then they get mad and resentful and critical and, well, they usually don't laugh.

Anyway, as this was happening on the set, despite my cautionary interruptions, I would eventually storm off, too angry to speak. I was not too angry to write, just too angry to let anyone hear what I was thinking because I didn't want to be barred from the stage. So, in an attempt to avoid a major conflict, I threw myself off the set.

Eventually, other problems took over and the picture finished shooting.

Then I went to the first screening and I wanted to… well, you know, slit my wrists while jumping out of the Empire State Building after taking an overdose of sleeping pills, hoping to land in front of a bus going, say, 150 miles an hour.

Because all the over-the-top stuff was in the film.

And I wanted to die.

But I was not ready to give up and I stood my ground. And I told the director that I thought we had made a mistake by trying the make the film tooooo funny. Since the first *Stakeout* had been moderately funny, we should attempt to follow that structure.

The director agreed. And he recut the film. And, by God, we

had a pretty nice picture. It had a tight dramatic structure with some comedy.

Then the test screenings began.

And each time the film got a laugh, it was decided that another laugh could be had, just with a little recutting and putting back some of the really funny stuff.

And I slowly watched as the pretty good film with dramatic structure and a little comedy became a comedy structure with a little bit of drama. But, dammit, I wasn't done slugging it out. I rolled up my sleeves, put in my mouthpiece, hiked up my shiny shorts and went back into the ring.

I called the studio head. He thought the picture was great, the consensus being that it's hard to argue when *the test screening numbers go up*.

I called the director. He thought the picture was great, too. After all, the *test screening numbers went up*.

I tried to argue that I didn't care what the test screening people thought. I didn't think the stuff in the film was funny. It didn't make me laugh. It made me cringe.

But… it's hard to argue with *the test screening numbers, especially when they go up!*

I called the star of the picture and I told him I thought we were destroying the movie by putting all the over-the-top stuff back into the film just because it got some laughs in the test screening. I told him I didn't think it was funny. It was silly.

And he said, "We're not making Shakespeare."

I thought to myself, is he accusing me of *not* stealing Shakespeare?

Well, I was offended. I quickly thought to myself. If I confessed that I had stolen the plot from Shakespeare, would that change his mind? I frantically went through the plots in my mind… *Romeo and Juliet*, no, *King Lear*, no, *Hamlet*… a stretch… Then I ran out of time. The star had to go.

I quickly yelled into the phone, "I have a confession to make…" But the line went dead.

And I had no one left to turn to. I was a lone voice in the wilderness. An outcast. A nobody.

And the film came out and it did a little business. And the studio and all involved were disappointed in the returns.

And what most people complained about was that the film wasn't as funny as it could have been.

Oh… what do I know? I'm only the writer.

Ahh, well, actually, I was also the producer.

A lot of good that did me.

# Sherwood Schwartz

## Pushing The Envelope

---

*"'Could you make it say something without changing it?'"*

Sherwood Schwartz created, wrote and produced the *Gilligan's Island* pilot. He also co-wrote (with George Wyle) the *Gilligan* theme song. He created, wrote and produced *The Brady Bunch* pilot and co-wrote *the Brady Bunch* theme (with Frank DeVol). He has received five WGA nominations and one award. He has been nominated for two Emmy® awards and won one.

Many years ago, I was producing *The Brady Bunch* series at Paramount. I was rewriting an episode when I got a call from a Paramount executive. He told me Paramount just sold a new comedy series for the fall to one of the networks. It had a 13-week commitment and everybody was very excited about it. I congratulated him. Then he asked if I would please take a look at the pilot. "It's only a half-hour," he added. He would set up one of the smaller viewing rooms for me.

It seemed like a curious request because he said everybody loved it just the way it was. Why did he need my opinion, I wondered. But I said, "Okay." Then he added, "I'd like you to view this by yourself." That made his request seem even more curious.

Anyway, I went to see the pilot and I called him afterward. He asked me what I thought of it. I said, "It's a funny pilot. Is there some kind of problem?"

"In a way," he answered.

"What way?" I asked.

And he said, "I just have a vague feeling it could be a little better. What do you think?"

"Anything can be a little better," I temporized.

"Of course," he agreed. "But I'm not sure it has legs."

And I said, "Well, it's very funny, but it really doesn't have anything to say, some significance. It would be better as a series if there were some cake under the whipped cream; or as the French might say, if it had a 'raison d'etre.' The Brady Bunch is a family comedy too, but it's about something that's happening now in our society, about two families becoming one family."

"Maybe that's what I mean," he said. "Maybe that would make it better; if it had something to say. Is there any way to do that with this show?"

"You mean a rewrite?"

"No, no, no. The network loves the show just the way it is. Could you make it say something without changing it?"

"Well, it's hard to change something without changing it."

"Would you think about it?" he asked. "Maybe that's what's troubling me, that it doesn't really have significance. That would give it more legs, if it had something to say."

I'm not sure if he realized how difficult that might be, to do a rewrite without doing a rewrite. But he was a nice guy and I liked it at Paramount, so I told him I would give it a shot. Sometimes things are easier than you think; sometimes they're harder than you think; and sometimes they're just plain impossible.

I returned to my office and I started to think about it, and this was one of those once-in-a-lifetime occasions. It turned out to be absolutely simple. It only took about half an hour to put my thoughts on paper.

My approach didn't change the story. It didn't change the characters. It didn't even change any of the scenes. The only thing it changed was the husband's job.

Then I phoned the executive and I told him I had an idea that might work.

He said, "Great. Can you get right over here?"

I said, "Sure." A few minutes later, I was in his office with an envelope containing two-and-a-half typewritten pages.

He said, "How did you solve the problem?"

I said, "It's right here in this envelope. It's only two or three pages." I pushed the envelope towards him across his desk.

Before he even touched it, he said, "Remember, they love the pilot just the way it is, so I hope you didn't really change anything."

"No, I really didn't change anything, except I gave it, as you put it, 'legs'."

"I don't want to look like a fool," he said. "I told them the pilot was great and they agreed the pilot was great, so I can't tell them it has to be changed to make it better."

I said, "Why would you be reluctant to tell them you've made it better? As a writer, I've been making things better all my life. That's what I'm doing here now."

"Well, they might lose confidence in me." he answered. "I told them the pilot was great just the way it was." He pushed the envelope back towards me.

I said, "Look, I didn't call you, you called me and you said something was troubling you. Maybe this change will make you feel better about the pilot." I pushed the envelope back towards him. "See for yourself."

He thought a moment and then he said, "What if I really like this change, and I really recommend it? I'd be crazy to make waves when they like it just the way it is." And he pushed the envelope back to me.

"I can just tear it up right now," I said. I picked up the envelope to tear it. "All I know is that if someone told me how to improve a story or a scene or a line, I would be happy to make the change. And I would thank him for the suggestion."

"You're right. Let me have that envelope."

I pushed the envelope back towards him.

Before he opened it, he said, "I'm not sure they would understand the significance of the kind of idea you're talking about. It might unravel all the work we've done selling them this pilot. It's just too chancy."

He pushed the envelope back to me.

"Okay. It doesn't make any difference to me one way or the other. I just thought it would make you a real hero if you told them you improved this pilot by making a tiny change that'll make their great pilot even greater. It can't hurt to take a look." And I pushed the envelope back to him.

He said, "We do business with the networks all the time. So it's not just this project. Anything in the future might be at risk if I guess wrong on their reaction to this idea."

This man was truly in such agony about making a simple decision, I was sorry I got the idea. Without realizing it, I had placed him in the worst possible position of any executive. He didn't care about being a hero. He was just terrified at the prospect of being wrong to begin with. He pushed the envelope back to me, and I decided to put an end to witnessing the meltdown of a really nice executive.

I took the envelope and left his office.

That unopened envelope still resides somewhere in the clutter of scripts for plays, movies, TV shows, outlines, letters, rewrites, etc., in the dusty depths of one of my closets.

P.S. That TV pilot went on the air exactly the way I had seen it in that small viewing room by myself. The series lasted 13 weeks, as per the guarantee.

# Winifred Hervey

## Now I Can Laugh, Too

---

*"We start shooting and soon realize that we're using up babies faster than we anticipated."*

Winifred Hervey has written for and created numerous half-hour comedies, but is best known for her work on *The Golden Girls*, *The Fresh Prince of Bel-Air* and *The Steve Harvey Show*. A single mother of two teenagers, she hopes to one day sleep in and date a man who doesn't have a great idea for a series.

I had just landed my first development deal and was to adapt a successful BBC half-hour comedy to an American sitcom. Along with the British creator and writer, I would produce and write the pilot based on his original series about a young working couple faced with the unplanned birth of a child. Her mother, a prim, high-strung, divorced blue blood, and his father, a hard-drinking, unemployed, working-class widower, share the flat downstairs from the couple and look after the child. During the pitching process, I notice that whenever the British writer speaks, everyone thinks every single word he says is absolutely brilliant. And I'm no chopped liver. It's the accent. Let's face it. Even the most mundane sounds smarter with a British accent. Take aluminum for example. We immediately decide he should do all the talking.

We sell the idea and have a blast writing it. The network loves it. Then we get the phone call. The network wants to use an all-black cast and make the baby triplets. Suddenly, it's not politically correct for both male characters to be unemployed and drinking. This means a major rewrite. After I scrape the British writer off the ceiling, I explain to him that in Hollywood, this is what they do when they like you. We now have one week to rehearse before we shoot the pilot. In that week, two lead actors in the four-actor ensemble are fired. The director barely escapes the same fate. We hire three sets of newborn triplets and a couple of backups, which means by law we are required to have a nursery, nurse and social workers. Our lighting director can light everything except the actors. The day we shoot, the lead actor comes in swollen and whacked out on painkillers. It seems he decided to have a root canal that morning. Do we shoot? Do we not shoot? By now, both the British writer and I just want the damn thing shot so it can be over.

We start shooting and soon realize that we're using up babies faster than we anticipated. We start scouring the city for more triplets. Our lead actor is freaking out, which throws off our new actress and flusters the director who, to our horror, cannot speak when flustered. The lighting is film noir sitcom. The actors playing the young couple decide they can no longer contain their lust for each other and start making out in front of the audience. We have to roll in a screen to block the view. Our back-up babies, who are driving in from Long Beach, have a breakdown on the freeway. We send a limo. The studio head has literally growled at me and the network guys won't look us in the eye. Finally, the babies show up just as the British writer quits. My producer, an editor and I begin the editing process in a tiny trailer. Before we can finish, we are not picked up. Later, several network executives joke about how much they botched things up. Now I can laugh about it, too. I can't speak for the British writer.

# Chris Brancato

## The Cat Stays In The Picture

*"We write because we dream."* Chris Brancato has written the feature screenplays *Hoodlum* and *Species II*. He created The Sci-Fi Channel's long-running television series *First Wave*. He's also written and/or produced numerous television shows, including *Beverly Hills 90210*, *The X-Files*, *The Outer Limits*, *Boomtown* and *North Shore*.

I sat in the cutting room at MGM as the final reel of *Species II* played on an editing machine. Hunched over the machine was none other than the Studio President. Here I was, the lowly writer, debating the final cut with the President of MGM, a studio with a proud history.

I'd been hired to script the sequel to the MGM hit film Species, written by Dennis Feldman. For those unaware, *Species* detailed the emergence on earth of Sil: a half-human, half-alien beauty whose danger lay in procreation. If you fell into her libidinous clutches, the resultant offspring could well destroy the planet Earth.

My sequel centered on Patrick Ross, a heroic astronaut infected with alien DNA on mankind's first mission to Mars. In order to stop Patrick's rampant sexual congress with adoring groupies, the U.S. government uses a laboratory clone of the original Sil (now named "Eve") to hunt down and kill Patrick before his offspring spell doom for the planet.

In my script, Eve defeats Patrick in a furious battle, though she too is killed. The wrap-up scene of *Species II* is the burial of Patrick. In a classic government cover-up, he's buried with full military honors. The public will never know how close it came to being alien puppy chow.

Back to the MGM cutting room, where the President announced that three of his previous movies ended in funerals. They all flopped at the box office. Though these movies were wholly unrelated to *Species II*, a funeral scene ending is a no-no. We will have to reshoot.

I dutifully went home to write a new ending. In the climactic battle of *Species II*, Eve and Patrick engage in a fight to the death. Like a praying mantis, Eve *may* have reproduced with her male counterpart prior to ripping out his lungs. Both Patrick and Eve are killed in the battle, but the question remains: was Eve impregnated? If so, the offspring would be twice as powerful as any alien seen before.

My new ending featured Eve's body in a military ambulance. She lies peaceful in death. As the ambulance engine rumbles, there's a vague tremor beneath the sheet that covers her body. With growing horror, we realize what has happened. Eve *has* been impregnated, and even though she's dead, the alien physiology is such that she will give birth to a lethal offspring. As her belly grows and grows, gestation on fast forward, we cut to black. End of movie.

On to *Species III*.

I faxed my new scene to the President's office and nervously awaited a response. Many hours and cups of coffee later, the phone rang. It was the President himself. "Loved that scene," he said. "Only one change. When we see Eve's been knocked up, let's pan to the corner of the ambulance and see one of Patrick's half-human, half-alien kids sitting in the corner."

With great deference, I suggested that the alien offspring had been eradicated by our heroes earlier in the picture. To have an alien "lovechild" in the ambulance would suggest that our heroes had been unsuccessful in their job. A screw-up of possibly world-ending proportions.

"Hey, there were at least thirty alien offspring in the picture," he argued. "Anyone could've missed one of those things. Not even Michael Madsen is perfect."

I hung up the phone. Demoralized. But soon my spirits lifted. I would call my Producer. Surely he'd protect my scene from this harebrained idea.

The Producer answered the phone curtly: "Loved your scene." Music to my ears. I told him about the alien love child suggested by the MGM President. "That's the dumbest thing I ever heard," he said. I agreed with great relief.

"But," he continued, "I've got a better idea."

My blood ran cold.

"When I produced *Friday the 13th Part VIII*," the Producer said, "the director had this cat jump into frame in the house where Jason was hiding. The audience in the test screening nearly pissed their pants."

I waited, not daring to breath.

"How about when we see Eve's belly growing, suddenly— whoosh—a cat jumps into frame."

"How'd a cat get into a military ambulance?" I asked.

But the Producer wasn't fettered by logic.

"It's in the woods," he cried. "Cats live in the woods!"

The Producer told me to call the President and tell him about the cat. "No matter what that jerk says," my Producer warned, *"the cat stays in the picture."*

I dejectedly called the President and told him about the cat. "Dumbest idea I ever heard," he said. I agreed, but suggested we drop the alien love child and hope the cat had the same effect on our audience that it did in *Friday the 13th Part VIII.* "No," said the President in a tone that reminded me of the ease with which writers get replaced, *"the alien love child stays in the picture."*

We write because we dream. We write because ink flows from our pens like blood in our veins. We write because we've been fired from every other useful occupation we've ever had. But to make a living as a writer is to accept the compromises that come in a collaborative medium. Most of the time, collaboration raises your work to a higher level. But not always.

In the end, the cat stayed in the picture.

But so did the alien love child. They both got their way, and I got writing credit on one of the dumbest scenes in modern film history. If you're catatonically depressed and in need of a chuckle, I suggest you rent a copy of *Species II* and fast forward to the final scene. Given the box-office tally of this movie, MGM could use the rental fee.

# Lewis Colick

## How *October Sky* Finally Achieved Liftoff

*"I was rewarded with every writer's dream—sitting in a theater and watching a movie you put your heart into, beautifully realized by a talented director and his team of gifted artists."*

Lewis Colick has written numerous films including *October Sky*, which was awarded the Humanitas Prize and was nominated for a Writers Guild award. He maintains that his Brooklyn upbringing made him ideally suited to write a movie about kids growing up in a West Virginia coal-mining town.

Back in 1998, I was having a meeting with a producer, who'd formerly been president of production at one of the majors. When I told him that I had a movie in production, he said great, what's it about. I told him that it was a true story about these kids from a poor coal-mining town, who, inspired by Sputnik, began building their own rockets. Against incredible odds, these boys won the national science fair, received college scholarships, and escaped the harsh life of coal mining to which they'd all seemed destined. The producer looked at me like I was full of shit, and practically laughed out loud as he asked the obvious question, "Who's making that?" I completely understood his stunned response. As a former studio head, he had a hard time believing that one of the majors was actually going to finance a film with so much going against it. I mean, come on... a small, period drama with no big stars and little appeal to the youth market? I was having a hard time believing it myself. So how did *October Sky* get made anyway?

Producer Chuck Gordon had come to me about a year earlier with a book proposal for a work in progress called *Rocket Boys*. Even in its earliest stages, the material was beautiful, compelling and inspiring, but I figured that getting a studio to pay me to adapt a film that would be small and period and a drama with no stars, etc., etc., would be next to impossible. But the Seagram family had just bought Universal Studios, where Chuck had his deal. The studio was flush with cash and eager to buy properties to put into development. They bought the book for me to adapt, and some months later, we turned in the script for *October Sky*. There was one problem. Universal's president of production, the guy who'd hired me, was now gone, replaced by a new team, and although they liked the script, they were, understandably, not jumping up and down about doing a picture that was small and period and a drama and had no stars, etc., etc. Chuck was told that the only way they'd get behind this project would be if he could attach a director who could give them "some degree of comfort." In other words, they wanted one of those big, commercial, heavyweight, impossible-to-get-because-everybody-in-town-wants-him directors. Guys like Spielberg and Zemeckis. And so Chuck submitted his list of names and the studio signed off on it, saying, in effect, get us one of these guys and we'll make your movie. Well, lo and behold, Chuck got them one of those guys. Knowing that director Joe Johnston, who'd made several huge, commercial hits like *Jumanji* and *Honey, I Shrunk The Kids*, was looking for a smaller, more personal type of film to direct, Chuck gave him the script and Joe took to it immediately. Chuck and I couldn't have been happier. There was just one problem. Joe's interest in little *October Sky*, it seemed, took the folks at Universal completely by surprise. They had been counting on Joe to direct a different picture for them—*The Incredible Hulk*. They saw *The Hulk* as a big summer picture, a tent-pole picture, an event picture, and Joe Johnston was the man they wanted. Naturally, I figured that *October Sky* was dead in the water. But Joe told Universal he didn't want to direct *The Incredible Hulk*; he wanted to direct *October Sky*. The studio was thrown by this, but valuing their relationship with Joe, made him a simple proposal—if he would first direct *The Incredible Hulk*, he could then direct *October Sky*. When I heard about this, I was thrilled. Sure, we'd have to wait a year, but at least *October Sky*—the long shot to end all long shots—would get made. But to everybody's surprise, Joe said no. He didn't want to direct *The Incredible Hulk*. And so, once again, I figured we were finished. But I was wrong. The studio came back to Joe with yet another proposal—if Joe would be willing to supervise a first-time director through production on *The Incredible Hulk*, then, with their blessings, he could go off and make *October Sky*. I was elated. Surely Joe would be willing to go for this. But he didn't. Joe just didn't want anything to do with *The Incredible Hulk*. In conveying the news, my agent told me, she doubted *October Sky* would ever get made at Universal.

And yet, of course, it did. Chuck prevailed upon the chairman of the studio to read the script while flying to New York. The chairman read it and he cried on the plane. And so with Joe Johnston providing the much needed "comfort level," he agreed to green light *October Sky*. Some months later, I was rewarded with every writer's dream—sitting in a theater and watching a movie you put your heart into, beautifully realized by a talented director and his team of gifted artists.

So how did *October Sky* get made? Simply put, I guess, it was because Joe liked the script.

# SECRETS OF THE HOLLYWOOD PROS #4:

## Tales From the Script Police

Because getting a script sold has become such a Sisyphian task, writers seldom ask what happens if you actually succeed in rolling the rock to the top of the hill. Be warned: when you get there, you may get pulled over by the script police, who're just waiting to bust you for failure to communicate.

Script supervisor Carol De Pasquale has policed films as diverse as *Smooth Talk, Runaway Bride, The Matrix Reloaded* (the U.S. 2nd Unit) and *The Princess Diaries* and *The Princess Diaries 2: Royal Engagement*. She warns that after you make it to the mountaintop of getting your script the green light, there is yet another mountain to climb called getting your vision on the screen. She offers a half-dozen "Do's and Don'ts" from her years on script patrol:

I have read a lot of scripts in my time: some great, some stinkers. I can't say that I have read thousands, like a lot of Hollywood big shots, but I can say that 99% of the scripts I have read—for better or worse—have been made into films.

A Script Supervisor generally gets a script when it is green-lit and in preproduction. While working with a script during the preproduction and production of a film, I refer to myself as the "Script Police" or the "Logic Police." Details that may have been flawed or glossed over when the script was being pitched, packaged and sold must now be made practical—or be eliminated. Everything has to work. If you want your vision to make it to the screen, your script really needs to be bulletproof!

You can help yourself by checking for any obvious flaws in your work.

Here are some of my Do's and Don'ts for the screenwriter:

**Proof your script, reproof your script, re-reproof your script—and then have a reliable person also proof, reproof and re-reproof it.**

Even the best scripts can have inconsistencies. As scripts go through rewrites, one simple change in a story point often requires a string of changes throughout the balance of the script. Things as simple as names and event time frames need follow through. Not proofing makes the script come off as sloppy and leaves room for unintended interpretation.

**The tighter the story and the character development, the less chance of "on-set" changes.**

Vagueness is a breeding ground for changes to the final film—and not necessarily for the best. You're lucky to have gotten your script to this stage, but in production, your baby has new parents. Clarity in expressing your story and character development will insure that your adoptive parents will portray your vision. For example:

Let's say that you are in the middle of a script where you have already established that the leading female character is ready for a divorce. She is unhappy because her husband doesn't put any effort into doing things that will make her happy. In fact her husband, even after 18 years, doesn't get what she's really about. You want to write a montage sequence as he shops for an anniversary gift. Here are two examples of such a sequence: the first vague, the second clear and specific.

# Example #1:

INT. SHOPPING MALL – DAY
Montage of John going in and out of various shops buying gifts for his wife Tammy. He buys  unromantic and inappropriate anniversary gifts.

# Example #2:

INT. SHOPPING MALL – DAY
John walks through a crowd of shoppers, stopping in front of a candy shop window. He examines the pretty boxes of chocolates then moves away without entering. He does the same in front of a lingerie shop.

INT. APPLIANCE STORE – DAY
John examines various household and kitchen appliances. He looks at irons, pots and pans, vacuums, mops, blenders and televisions.

INT. GARDEN SHOP — DAY

John is at the checkout station purchasing a weed-whacker. Resting on the floor beside him as he pays are shopping bags containing boxes: a vacuum, an electric coffeepot and blender.

These examples are intentionally heavy-handed to illustrate a point. Don't assume that it is obvious that the most clueless gifts John could give his wife are related to housekeeping. If you don't spell it out in your script, you could end up seeing Tammy receiving frumpy clothes and tacky jewelry. Is that what you envisioned? Is that the way you imagined John to be clueless? Remember: character is in the details.

**Do your homework and get your facts straight.**

I ran into a simple plot flaw in a recent script I was prepping. In a climatic scene, an important character was on a mission to pick up some Federal Express packages from the post office on a holiday Saturday. My note was that Federal Express does not deliver to post offices. I also didn't really believe that the post office would be open on a big national holiday. When identifying a known entity like Federal Express, accuracy is required. Doing your homework will keep the Script Police from changing your script after it is out of your hands. As it turned out, the scene described was never shot. In fact, the whole sequence that built to this scene was implausible, cut in preproduction by the studio and rewritten.

**Don't write scenes that leave action or dialogue up to the actors unless this is your intent.**

**Here's a sample scene:**

> INT. LIBRARY – NIGHT
> Lillian sits with Anthony, explaining parliamentary procedure.

A more visual description that gives the actors something specific to do, without relying on ad-libbed dialogue, might read like this:

> INT. LIBRARY – NIGHT
> Lillian sits with Anthony at a dimly lit table stacked high with aged leather bound law books. She shows him various passages from several of the thickest books.

**Camera directions can be annoying.**

The fact is, the director and cinematographer are going to shoot their movie the way they see best. If you include dolly, zoom or slo-mo references, try to be sure that they truly add to the drama of the scene. Even then, there are no guarantees that they will be followed. There may be location or light limitations, as well as a different directorial creative vision. I also think phrases like "we see…" or "the camera moves in on…" generally pull the reader out of the story. This kind of writing is one of my pet peeves. For purposes of the best film, keep to the drama/story. Unless a camera direction is needed to make a story point, my experience is that directing the camera decreases the writer's odds for a true visual rendition of his or her creation.

**Use visual descriptions. Introducing a character with nonvisual background history is useless.**

**Here's another sample scene:**

INT. CLUB – NIGHT

The party was in full swing. Standing behind Joyce in the buffet line is DAVID PFIRMAN, a German, three-time Olympic gold medalist, whose devious uncle was the husband of the guest of honor.

Unless David is wearing his Olympic medals and speaks unscripted dialogue with a German accent as his uncle steals a piece of silver flatware, how is the audience going to get this information? More to the point, is David's background information important to the plot and/or his character? The audience can't read the script; so if the information is important, you need to come up with a nonliterary, cinematic way to impart the essential backstory. Often scripted "throwaway" dialogue comes off best and sounds less like "pipe" (nonvisual story point information).

**Here's a rewrite of the sample scene:**

INT. CLUB – NIGHT

The party was in full swing. Standing behind Joyce in the buffet line is an athletic-looking young German man, DAVID PFIRMAN. Joyce and David notice as an older gentleman, HENRY KLIEN, whispers to the head waiter and then hands him a hundred-dollar bill. The waiter quickly stashes the money into his pocket, nods knowingly and leaves.

DAVID (German accent)
Uncle Henry, what are you up to now?
Auntie is just about to be honored on stage.

HENRY (sarcastic; German accent)
David, you stick to winning your gold medals
and I'll mind my wife as I see fit!

Again, the example is heavy-handed. But then, I'm not a writer. You are. Do you want me rewriting your script?

In my experience, a script has its best chance of being true to the writer's vision if it is written so as not to need a preproduction fix. Production is specific. But don't overdo details; be in control of the details so that you marshal the ones that paint the picture you want to create. When a script has to be changed during preproduction, whether to create specifics or to maintain logic and continuity, it often leads to a writer's worst nightmare: a nonwriter fixing a problem on the day of shooting, on the set. And believe me, it happens.

So when writing, try to imagine each element up on the silver screen. Hook your audience early. Write what you know—and if you don't know enough, do your research. Think visually. If you can, say it in pictures rather than words. With dialogue, less is often more. Question the truthfulness of your characters. Don't risk unintended directorial consequences. Make what you write shootable. When in doubt, triple-proof yourself and then get someone else to do the same. And most of all, don't try to fit into someone else's mold: have fun writing something of your own. Good luck!"

# BONUS SECRET OF THE HOLLYWOOD PROS #2:

## Protection So You Don't Get Screwed

There's lots of nasty stuff going around Hollywood, like idea theft. It could be fatal to your project. So, if you're gonna write—and I hope you're gonna—you need to write safely. You need protection.

How do you protect your script, treatment, synopsis or idea?

Register it with the Writers Guild of America.

Here's how it works: by registering your material, you create evidence of the legal existence of a piece of work as of the date of registration. The Writers Guild Intellectual Property Registry, as a neutral third party, can testify to that evidence.

Here's what you don't get: a guarantee that someone won't try to screw you anyway. Think about it: do condoms prevent bad relationships? Does that mean you shouldn't use one?

To register your material, you don't have to be a member of the Guild. You don't have to be in Los Angeles. You don't even need a script. Any writer can register treatments, stories and outlines in addition to scripts and other intellectual property over the Internet for a small fee (currently $10 for WGA members in good standing; $20 for anyone else). For more information, visit www.wga.org and follow the link: Register Your Script.

And remember: when it's time to show your work, be careful out there.

*"You have all the scenes. Just go home and word it in."*
—Samuel Goldwyn to Billy Wilder and I.A.L. Diamond

# Chapter 5

## INTRODUCTION

## Collaboration:

## I Did it Their Way

---

It used to be that the status of writers in Hollywood could be summed up in the old joke about the ambitious starlet, who was under contract to a major studio, who was so dumb that when she heard that the way to get ahead in the business was to screw a writer, she screwed *all* the writers on the lot, just to be safe.

While it's doubtful writers were ever really that powerless—or, sadly, starlets that obliging—it is no doubt true that the relationship between writers and our other collaborators in the collaborative art of filmmaking has always been—to use the language of contemporary relationship psychology—fraught with issues.

Under the old studio system, the issue was being a cog in the machine. Eight studios owned everything: every element of production— screenplay, actors, sets—as well as every element of distribution/ exhibition, aka, the movie theatres.[4] But most

4. The Big Eight oligarchy consisted of five fully vertically-integrated companies that owned production, distribution and exhibition entities: Paramount, MGM-Loew's, Warner Bros., RKO and 20th Century Fox; and three partially integrated companies that controlled production and distribution but were not in the theater business: Universal, Columbia and United Artists.–Ed.

---

importantly, they owned you. They told you what to write and how to write it. They were cranking out movies like they were Model Ts; and the writer's job was to create the right vehicle for each of the studio's stars. Down one assembly line came a "Frankly, my dear, I don't give a damn" for Clark Cable; down another, a "Nyack, nyack, nyack" for the Three Stooges; down still another, a "Sufferin' Succotash" for a certain little black duck. Unlike the literal assembly lines of Detroit, however, which were governed by union work rules, the Hollywood dream factory was ruled by the autocratic whims of the studio heads. Not only were salaries and working conditions arbitrary, writing credit sometimes didn't go to the writers but to relatives and paramours of the powerful.

Writers fought back by unionizing. In 1937, the Screen Writers Guild—which had begun in 1921 as a kind of glorified social club, complete with a clubhouse!—was certified by the National Labor Relations Board as a bona fide collective bargaining unit. In 1939, bargaining began; and the first contract with the studios was signed in 1942. In gaining the power to decide who got credit for any produced screenplay—one of the significant provisions of the first contract—writers gained recognition of an inherent principle: that movies are made from screenplays and writers author those screenplays. Under the Work for Hire doctrine first articulated in the Copyright Act of 1909, the studios are the "authors" for the purpose of copyright—and the argument continues to this day over whether an employee or independent-author model best serves writers. But, there is no question that when a legal tsunami swept away the old studio system, writers found new ways to marshal the power of authorship to reinvent themselves as risk-taking entrepreneurs, especially in television.

That tsunami emanated from the Supreme Court. In its 1948

decision in the antitrust case begun ten years earlier against the motion picture cartels, United States v. Paramount, the court laid out a legal regime for the separation of ownership of production, distribution and exhibition of movies. In plain language, the court opined that you can make movies or you can exhibit movies, but you can't do both. The Court's "just say 'no' to vertical integration" stance—coupled with technology-driven changes in consumer demand wrought by the new medium of television—put a stake through the heart of the old studio system. Some studios, like RKO and United Artists, began a slow and painful death that played out over the next several decades. Others, like Universal, under the leadership of Lew "The Last Mogul" Wasserman, found new life in the television business. What this meant for writers was that the screenplay began to emerge as one of the new organizing principles of the business: "It's the material, stupid."

In movies, there is no more important early example of the power of material than the "spec" sale in the late Sixties of a Western screenplay with a hip, au courant attitude, written by a young novelist turned screenwriter who modestly claimed that he was still figuring out how to write a screenplay: William Goldman. *Butch Cassidy & The Sundance Kid*, which sold for the then-unheard of sum of $400,000, attracted one of the biggest stars of the era, Paul Newman (who had attached himself to the script prior to its sale), vaulted the then-unknown Robert Redford (who had replaced Steve McQueen in the package after negotiations with Warren Beatty failed) into international stardom, and remains one of the most financially and artistically successful films of all time. Writers began to initiate the process of making films by writing or pitching the movies they wanted to see. Writing became the well-spring of a renaissance of American film, led by hyphenate "auteurs" like Woody Allen, Francis Ford Coppola, George Lucas and Steven Spielberg who, though known as directors, saw themselves as writers first. That flowering created an emerging class of superstar writers like William Goldman, his brother Bo, Frank Pierson and Robert Towne.

On the increasingly financially lucrative and creatively daring television side of the business, visionary writer-show creators functioning as independent producers—such as William Link and Richard Levinson, creators of *Columbo* and *Murder, She Wrote*—became powerful. Writer-driven companies like the legendary MTM studios— home of James L. Brooks, Steven Bochco, Allan Burns and an incubator for a generation of others like Stephen J. Cannell Productions and Spelling/Goldberg Productions—became the networks' "go-to guys" for television programming. Each top company possessed a distinct "voice," which the companies sought to cultivate because they made serious money selling their "brand" to the networks, even as they simultaneously pushed the envelope in order to stay creatively fresh. Thus, MTM, the house of smart and human comedy like *The Mary Tyler Moore Show*, found new horizons by also becoming the house of smart and human drama like *St. Elsewhere* and *Hill Street Blues*.

The growing power of writers was tracked by advances in the WGA contract with the studios and networks (secured through difficult but ultimately successful strikes): residuals, health & pension, creative rights and guarantees of copyright-like ownership rights in future revenue streams from their creations ("separated rights" is the term of art for this guarantee).

Writers were still getting screwed, but the price of screwing them had gone way up.

As writers enjoyed an expansion of their power in the wake of the organizational Wild West left by the demise of the studio system, a new sheriff decided to clean up the town: the agent.

Simply put, agents like Stan Kamen at William Morris and Mike Ovitz and his partners at the fledgling Creative Artists Agency figured out that what Goldman had achieved with *Butch Cassidy & the Sundance Kid* was, in effect, a business plan. The screenplay became an essential organizing principal of the business because a great script attracts the other elements necessary to make a movie—director and, especially, stars—which can then be put up for auction to obtain production money.

If you control the package, the studio comes to you. Who needs to own a bunch of real estate with a fancy gate?

Way before the Internet age of virtual reality, big packaging agencies became virtual studios. Meanwhile, studio lots became movie motels, renting out high-priced production space and facilities to all comers, including their own productions. Because packaging pushed up the cost of making movies through escalating talent costs—while budgets were being busted by the astronomical production costs of special-effects-driven "event" movies that began with the seminal success of *Star Wars* and *Jaws*—studios began to hedge their financial bets by eschewing complete ownership of "their" movies in favor of spreading the risk through investor partnerships.

Packaging induced a similar rise in the cost of television production. When coupled with the clout of writer-driven independent producers at the networks, rising costs pushed the studios into the position of deficit financers of television programs, making up the difference between what the networks paid for programming (the "license fee") and the true cost of making the program (the "deficit") in return for profit participation in syndication ("reruns"). On the small screen, the MTM kitty was pushing the MGM lion off the screen, while on the big screen, the big cat had to share screen time with the names of arcane limited partnerships that sounded as likely to be in the money-laundering business as the movie business.

But at the end of the Eighties, a new era in Hollywood was about to open, starring the monster that ate Hollywood and had come back for another helping: *Vertical Integration: the Sequel.*

After the "success" of deregulation in other industries, like the airline and interstate bus industries, the FCC was under pressure to deregulate movies, television and radio. Their conflict-of-ownership rules—the Fin-Syn Rules, as in Financial Interest/Syndication Rules, which maintained that you can produce a television show or you can broadcast it, but you can't do both—were in the center of the deregulation bull's-eye. The networks, whose income came from advertising revenue generated in a show's initial run (not reruns), argued that Fin-Syn unfairly cut them out of the unending syndication profit stream flowing from the ownership of TV shows. To no one's surprise, the studios argued that they, too, were being unfairly cut out of the same profit stream by Fin-Syn's prohibition against owning both television shows and the networks that broadcast them.

In 1991, the FCC liberalized the Fin-Syn rules, unleashing a new wave of vertical integration, beginning with television. Taking the first chomp, the networks began producing their own shows. The studios howled in protest, all the way to the U.S. Court of Appeals. In 1995, the Court of Appeals relaxed the rules out of existence by siding with 20th Century Fox, which was trying to become a TV network and a studio (apparently taking its cue from the old TV commercial: "It's a network. It's a studio. Stop! You're both right!") It's no coincidence that 1995 was the year that Fox's competitor, Disney, went out and bought a network, Cap Cities/ABC. It's also no coincidence that there are now five major networks, each of which is owned by one of the five major studios. And it's also no coincidence that most of the shows you see on the networks are produced and owned by the network or their parent company studio or that the mascot of the Association of Independent Television Producers is the dodo.[5]

How have writers responded to this? The truth is: we're still figuring it out.

The good news is that writers' incomes are up. The bad news is that earning that higher income is becoming harder. At posh Westside watering holes and garden parties in the Palisades, self-satisfied banter about how the seller's market in real estate values has caused home prices to go through the roof has been replaced by genuine angst over how the buyer's market in Hollywood has made it nearly impossible to get a movie made or a show on the air.

So what does all this have to do with *moi*, you say? Though I believe that a writer's first obligation is to the writer's vision—that which we believe and feel most deeply in our hearts and minds— the practical work of a writer in Hollywood doesn't exist in a vacuum. We are part of an industry. And the state of that industry is always the 800-pound gorilla in any writing room. When I began, I was advised to read the trades to keep up with the business. Today, I advise you to read the trades and the business sections of the national newspapers.

But as important as rumination may be on the rise and fall and rise of corporate power in Hollywood, the irony remains that writers still retain the greatest power of all: we have the first word.

And, as our next essays prove, we also have the last word.

And... the last laugh.

5. This is a joke: there is no AITP. But you get the point.

# Joseph Stefano

## A Fifty-Plus Year Career As A Writer/Producer

*"By fearless, I mean unafraid to deal with the writer of this screenplay they liked enough to sign on for."*

Joseph Stefano is a former songwriter who is the screenwriter of *Psycho*, the co-creator and producer/writer of *The Outer Limits* and author of the original screenplays *The Black Orchid* and *Two Bits*. He's now working on another original, *Cielo Drive*, and still writes songs—for his wife's entertainment.

Writing your screenplay is the lovely, harmless part.

It's through the game that follows—I call it Heaven or Hell—that you learn what the movie business is all about. Heaven, if you have Alfred Hitchcock directing, as I did. Hell, if you wind up with a self-imagined director who changes your screenplay until it's unrecognizable or, worse, one who shoots it exactly as written but gets it all wrong.

I've had the good fortune to work with a few fearless directors throughout my career. By fearless I mean unafraid to deal with the writer of this screenplay they liked enough to sign on for. I mean not intimidated by having the writer on the set. I mean knowing and respecting the meaning of the word "collaboration." My first screenplay, *The Black Orchid*, was in the rough, sweet hands of Martin Ritt. If I'd been homeless, Marty would've let me sleep on his set.

Good fortune is too mild a phrase to explain getting my second film. I mean, Hitchcock didn't even want to meet with me. But my great agent Ned Brown was determined, and all of MCA, on both coasts, worked with him. Hitchcock caved, very likely just to get them off his back. He had his office send me a book, *Psycho*, by Robert Bloch. A meeting was set. Hitchcock, Ned, me. Things were said at that meeting that got me the assignment.

Working with Hitchcock was the kind of education no film school can provide. He knew—and shared with me—everything one ought to know to make movies. He also involved me in all preproduction matters and gave me a shoot-long invitation to his set. (I'll say little more about my experience with him, because I've written a play about the joys and horrors of being in Freudian analysis and going directly from that couch on Bedford Drive to the one in Hitchcock's Paramount office to work on a movie about—of all things!—a Mom Killer.)

The writer in me is proudest of my work on *The Outer Limits*, the sci-fi anthology series I co-created with my late friend Leslie Stevens. I consider it the centerpiece of my career and believe that producing it and writing 12 of the episodes might not have been quite so possible—and lasting—had I not worked with Alfred Hitchcock on *Psycho* and *Marnie*. Almost all of my episodes were directed by Gerd Oswald, a man whose genius and daring and dearness of heart made him one of the greats. I miss him more severely with each new project I take on.

I'm happy to say that the younger directors I've worked with the last couple of decades, such as Stephen Carpenter, Doug Adams, Mick Garris, exhibited the almost extinct ability to look upon the screenwriter as a collaborator. Same can be said for Gus Van Sant, a delight to work with despite his refusal to let me rewrite a scene in *Psycho* that has been often (and rightly) criticized.

All in all, I have been helped by directors far more than hurt by them. But hurt I've been. Ineffably. Consider this penultimate paragraph a cautionary tale:

A screenplay I'd written in the early '60s went into production in the early '90s. It had taken years to find the right producer and more years to find a director after our original choice, Martin Ritt, died. The director we wound up with seemed humane. He came to my house, enjoyed the patio lunch my wife Marilyn served, discussed the script. He wanted no changes. (He claimed to be the catalyst that had brought us the star, but, later, someone more likely to have done so claimed that credit.) The pain began long before Day One of the shoot. He excluded me from all discussions except those specifically named in my contract with the producer. When I arrived on the set the first day, he would not look at me or speak to me; this behavior continued throughout the shoot. The worst of it all? His cut turned out so lugubriously bad that the releasing company took over with its famous scissorhands, adding narration to fill in the holes. (Surprisingly, I was permitted to write the narration.) The released version was not an improvement. My heart broke. (I'll share a secret with you: This screenplay was the only one I had dared hope might get me an Oscar® nomination.)

I might've retired after that whammy. But three things happened. Marilyn told me she was not ready for me to be retired. Gus Van Sant asked me to work with him on his remake of *Psycho*. And, a new millennium dawned. So, I'm still in the business I love more than I hate and in which I've had more joy than heartbreak. And I've never felt happier or healthier or (dare I say it?) younger.

# Luisa Leschin

## Pitching Curve Balls

*"Because that's what writers do: we make things up out of thin air."*

A former professional ballet dancer, actor and voice-over artist, Luisa Leschin has co-authored two award-winning plays, *Latins Anonymous* and *The La La Awards*. She has also written for feature film, animation and television, including *Resurrection Blvd.* and *The George Lopez Show*, where she is supervising producer.

I owe my writing career to Speedy Gonzalez.

Just when I had decided I was going to treat my writing as a hobby—only writing what I was moved to write and not expecting to make a living at it—I got a panicked call from my friend who worked at Warner Bros. Animation. "I'm desperate and you're Latina. You have to help me on this project. The WB is considering using Speedy Gonzalez as the station's logo, but they're worried he's politically incorrect. We have to rehabilitate Speedy's image." Who could say no to that challenge?

We worked hard updating Speedy's brazero outfit, suggested Antonio Banderas to voice his "Andale, Epales" and wrote him a fun treatment for a movie that would launch his career again. In the end, the WB went with Michigan J. Frog. But for me, I had my first "legitimate" writing credit. Okay, I had a weird writing credit for a legitimate company.

So, when I got a meeting with Universal for an open writing assignment for a feature, I walked in with my head high. After all, this is a business of agreement and clearly someone at Warner Bros. Animation had thought enough of my talent to give me a job. I met with two very nice executives who told me that this was a passion project for their boss. "Great, what is it?" This proved to be a difficult question because, they informed me, "Our boss doesn't communicate very well." After further prodding, I learned that Mr. Doesn't-Communicate-Well wanted a Latino-based movie with a musical component.

Oh-kay. That narrowed it down. Desperate to stay in the picture, I told the execs about a Latino-based sitcom I had with a strong dance component, which of course would include music. No one was biting. "The leads are a brother and sister." The executives' ears perked up. "Did you say brother and sister? Our boss mentioned something about a brother and sister." And just for saying those magic words, I made the cut over dozens of other writers.

When I came back for my meeting with Mr. Doesn't-Communicate-Well, I pitched the Latino-based, music-driven movie I had conceived with a brother and sister as the protagonists. "I like it," he said, "but what's with the brother and sister thing? I want passion and romance. Change that and you have a story. "Well no. Change that and I had nothing left of the original take. Of course, I went home and rewrote the entire pitch.

And this is where I hope I can save you from making the same fatal mistake I made as a rookie pitcher.

I came in for my third meeting. This was it. I was going to walk away with a writing assignment—or not. I was supremely prepared. I knew my story, my characters, and the tone of the piece. Everything was carefully rehearsed and memorized. After the mandatory pleasantries, I launched. "This story can be set in any city that has old, established, integrated neighborhoods like New York, Los Angeles or Miami." Now, I grew up in New York and knew a lot of Puerto Ricans, had lived in L.A. and hung out with a lot of Chicanos and Latinos, but I had never stepped foot in Cuban Miami. "Hell," said Mr. Doesn't-Communicate-Well, "let's set it in Miami, it's fun to shoot there."

Well, the good news is I got the job. But because of that slip, EVERYTHING had to change. I mean EVERYTHING. The characters were now first-, second- and third-generation Cubans walking the streets of Calle Ocho. The old timers reminisced about Havana and hated Fidel. And let's not forget the rhythm of Cuban dialect. I was given eight weeks to write the first draft and it took four weeks of research before I could write word one.

So, my first big-time writing job, I wrote about people I didn't know, living in a city I'd never been in, trying to break into an industry I had never been around. When I didn't kill myself and when I turned in a script that was praised for its "authenticity," I realized that, yes, I was a professional writer. Because that's what writers do: we make things up out of thin air.

# Ted Tally

## On Collaboration: Red Dragon

*"It's important that we all keep working hard to become full creative partners."*

Ted Tally is the author of five produced stage plays and eight produced movies, including *Silence of the Lambs*, *Red Dragon* and *White Palace*. His unproduced scripts fill a warehouse in Pasadena.

The phone rings at my Pennsylvania office. It's Brett Ratner, the director of *Red Dragon*. "Ted, hi, I'm calling from the set. I'm about to shoot one of Edward Norton's scenes. He wants to change a few words of dialogue from your screenplay, but I told him he'd have to discuss it with you. He's right here. I'll put him on."

Daydream? Screenwriter's fantasy? No, that actually happened during the intensely collaborative production of *Red Dragon*. Over a period of many months, in countless ways both large and small, I was always made to feel like a full creative partner on this project.

Believe me, that isn't something I take for granted. In fact, I've been in the business long enough now to have experienced, firsthand, just about every kind of humiliation that can be heaped on screenwriters. Failed collaborations usually involve egos that are monstrously oversized yet insecure. The writer, typically, is viewed as either a mere employee (the "word guy"), to be dispensed with once there's a script, or worse, is secretly feared as some sort of threat to the director's on-set authority or "vision."

Thus the screenwriter—the first, the only other person to see the entire movie in his head—is frequently wasted as a potential resource during the production. The result, almost inevitably, is a damaged movie. We've all seen it happen, and grousing about such things is practically our screenwriters' national anthem.

But it's important to remember that it doesn't have to be that way.

On *Red Dragon*, the producers, Dino and Martha De Laurentiis, invited me out to Los Angeles to meet with Brett before he was hired. It was crucial to them that I approve of him, too. They arranged dinner parties for me to get to know both him and the movie's stars. They faxed and e-mailed script suggestions (always suggestions, never demands), not only from themselves but also from the novel's author, Thomas Harris. They viewed me not just as a valuable resource, but as a colleague and friend. They spared no effort or expense to see that I was treated at all times with respect, courtesy, and affection by everyone at the studio and by everyone involved in the making of the movie.

They set the tone for the entire collaboration that followed.

The production designer, Kristi Zea, sent me sketches for the major sets, wanting my feedback but also knowing that having the visuals before me would help me as I revised action and dialogue. At another point, we talked at great length about the look and feel I had in mind for an especially important prop. A *prop*!

Brett sent me actors' auditions on tape, asking for my reactions. (*Auditions!*) I was flown out for the cast read-through, then flown out again repeatedly for set visits and consultations. When I couldn't be on the set, Brett frequently sent me dailies, again on tape. As longer scenes and sequences began to be assembled, he sent those, too. "Here are three differently edited versions of Scene 117. Tell me which one you like best and why." We talked almost daily on the phone and I was also encouraged to share my ideas with Andy Davis, our executive producer, and Mark Helfrich, our editor.

When it came time for the national and international press junkets, Universal Studios made sure that I was given just as much of a spotlight as the director, producers, and stars—all of whom repeatedly expressed, on TV and in print, their high regard for the screenplay. I gave scores of interviews 'til my head was spinning. (I almost began to feel nostalgic for the many times on other movies when I was ignored.)

You might be thinking, "Sure, they had to be nice to him; he wrote the screenplay for *The Silence of the Lambs*." But the fact is, I was treated with the same degree of respect and affection on that movie as well, 12 years ago, when I had no leverage at all— whereas most of my movies in-between have been a different, less happy story. So if there's some magic formula for triumphant collaborations, I've never been able to bottle it.

In the end, I think it comes down to character and to common sense. Directors, producers and movie stars—the ones who are really good—know that they didn't get there on their own. Screenwriters don't need their charity, just a healthy dose of mutual self-interest. Hey, guess what, Hollywood? We actually know a lot more about storytelling than "just" the words on the page. Why not use us?

It's important that we all keep working hard to become full creative partners. And when collaborations do work out successfully, as they did on *Red Dragon*, it's equally important to give our partners the credit they deserve.

(Reprinted from *Written By* magazine, December 2002/January 2003 issue.)

# Glenn Gordon Caron

## My First Time at the Table

*"What he did for me that day remains one of the kindest acts of professional courtesy and generosity I have experienced in my 20-some years in the business."*

Glenn Gordon Caron's work for television includes creating, writing and producing the television series *Moonlighting*, for which he won the Writers Guild Award, and *Medium*. In addition, he has created the genre-bending science-fiction series *Now and Again* and has directed such feature films as *Clean and Sober*, *Wilder Napalm*, *Love Affair* and *Picture Perfect*.

Back in 1979, at the ripe old age of 24, my wife and I left our studio apartment behind the Chelsea Hotel in New York for California, where I was to begin work on the television series *Taxi*. I loved *Taxi*. Still do. Recently saw the pilot again and it's still filled with great humor and a wonderful, scruffy audacity. My agents at ICM had somehow convinced the show's producers to offer me a contract to write five freelance episodes for the series which was just entering its second season. I had never worked on a television show, never lived in California, never made more than $180 a week. I was giddy.

With the considerable help of the Charles Brothers and Barry Kemp and the rest of the staff of the show, I wrote my first episode, which played quite successfully during "sweeps." I was on my way. Or so I thought. The phone call to begin work on the subsequent episodes never came and while no one offered an explanation, I surmised that perhaps my youthful enthusiasm did not really make up for my lack of experience, and the day I insisted that Alex Rieger "would not do that" in the middle of a story meeting and then went on for 45 minutes explaining why he "would not do that" (whatever "that" was) to the people who *created* Alex Rieger was probably ill-advised. I admired these people and their work so much (still do), the pain of not pleasing them sent me into a personal tailspin.

It was in the midst of this period of intense career reassessment ("Would you like fries with that burger?") when I received a phone call from Charles Joffe. Joffe was a producer who at that time was most famous for shepherding Woody Allen's films to the screen (he had just picked up an Oscar® for *Annie Hall*). He was also the principal in a management company that managed Allen, along with the young David Letterman, Robin Williams and pretty much everybody else who was funny at the moment. He explained that in addition to everything else he and his partners were doing, they wanted to be in the business of making television. To that end they had been working with a writer they believed to be a "genius." Would I like to meet him and perhaps become involved with his new series?

The writer was a fellow in his forties named Steve Gordon. And he really was a genius. He had come up through advertising and made a name for himself by writing an innovative and truly funny series of commercials for Barney's, the New York clothing retailer. He had just penned his first feature (*The One and Only*) and was now creating a dark and edgy three-camera comedy for television inspired largely by the *Sweet Smell of Success* called *Good Time Harry*.

And he wanted me to be his Story Editor. Oh joy! I was being given a second chance. Someone over at *Taxi* had actually said something positive on my behalf to Joffe, who had repeated it to Steve and Steve now wanted to hire me.

I jumped at the chance. And this time, I was to be part of the staff. And what a staff it was—in addition to Steve and myself, there would be Mickey Rose, Woody Allen's collaborator on *What's Up, Tiger Lily?*, *Take the Money and Run* and *Bananas*. I had died and gone to heaven. I would come in every day and drink coffee and eat bagels and talk sports and old movies and tell jokes and oh yeah, write! I had a desk and an IBM Selectric typewriter and access to a Xerox machine and a parking spot with my name on it. It was all I could do to keep from wetting myself.

Our initial order from NBC was for six episodes, with Steve expected to write the first four pretty much by himself. I was to write show five and Mickey was slated for show six. And so it began. Steve's episodes were great. Joffe was right. Steve *was* a genius. Each week as rehearsals would start, we would all sit there and think how lucky we were to be working on such a great show with such an inspired leader. Twenty years later, I can still remember whole scenes word for word. At the same time, I was slowly coming to realize that Steve's comic voice was *so* wildly unique that it would be all I could do to try and absorb enough of it to write my episode.

Finally, I handed it in. The following day, Steve called me into his office. "It's good."

That day—those two words—meant almost as much to me as my wife saying, "I do". I had pleased someone. I could write. I had earned the parking space, the bagels, the Selectric. The whole next week, I floated through the halls. I was a writer! And *another writer* liked what I wrote. Wow. Soon my script would go to the table. The cast would read it aloud. I would actually *hear* it read—that is, if my heart didn't stop beating from the sheer excitement of it all. I thanked Steve about a hundred times a day. I had never heard my words spoken by actors. On *Taxi*, I simply handed in my script and waited for it to show up on TV. By the time I saw it on television, so much of it had changed, it was hard to feel a real sense of authorship. But this would be different. I would *hear* my words. I would guide it through the rehearsal and performance process. My script was going to the table!

On table day, I made my way to the stage to join Steve, the studio and network executives and the cast. As I took my seat, I couldn't help but notice the grim expression on our Star and those seated around him. He asked for quiet and once he had it, he pushed my unopened script across the table like a plate of spoiled fruit and suggested strongly that to read it aloud would be a waste of his and his fellow actors' time. And after all, couldn't that time be better spent running the script through Steve's typewriter? Steve began to protest, but the other actors joined in.

I was taught in high school biology that breathing is an *involuntary* function, but at that moment, it was all I could do to remember to expel the air from my lungs shortly after I inhaled. The room began to spin and the prospect of pushing myself away from the table and making my way back to the office with Steve and the others seemed a physical impossibility. I don't think I looked up the entire length of the trek—just stared at my feet as I walked from one end of the lot to the other, the wooden floor of the stage giving way to the asphalt of the back lot, which finally became the carpeting of our offices.

Steve wordlessly indicated with his finger that I should follow him into his room and he shut the door behind us. I apologized profusely for letting him down, for taking up space, for presuming to be able to write what clearly only he could write. With a wave of his hand, he silenced me and told me to sit down. "I want you to hear it." I was baffled. Hadn't he listened to his actors? There was no way they were going to read my script. They hated it. He ignored me and called in his assistant. "We'll be putting out a new draft tomorrow morning. A blue draft." She asked when she could expect the changes. He explained that he would give them to her right now—there was really only one. It was on the title page. It should read "revised."

The next morning, we were back at the table. The reading went well. The entire cast commented how much better the script had become. Steve insisted that he hadn't done much—that I had made the lion's share of the changes myself. There was clearly work to do, but that was what the remainder of the week was for.

The episode turned out well. A month or so later, NBC relayed word back that Fred Silverman hated the show. Not my episode. Every episode. He scheduled it for 10:30 on Saturday night—the six episodes aired and were quickly forgotten. Steve said, "I'll show you," and went off and wrote and directed a hysterical little movie called *Arthur*. It was the second most popular film of that year after *Raiders of the Lost Ark*. A short time later, he died of a heart attack at the age of 46.

What he did for me that day remains one of the kindest acts of professional courtesy and generosity I have experienced in my 20-some years in the business. His encouragement came at a moment of acute professional uncertainty for me and in extending it, he risked losing the confidence of his cast, studio and network.

I miss him terribly.

# Winnie Holzman

## Room With A View

---

*"You decide to bring in more characters, to keep the characters you never understood in the first place company."*

Emmy® nominee Winnie Holzman created the television drama *My So-Called Life* and wrote the book for the Broadway musical *Wicked*, for which she was nominated for a Tony Award.

"That conference room is too small," you say to Ed Zwick and Marshall Herskovitz after the very first table read of your very first script of your third television series with them. "It's claustrophobic; can't we have the table reads somewhere else?" Ed looks deeply into your eyes and says something eloquent that has nothing to do with your question. Marshall looks at you with the same expression he's looked at you with for the past 12 years—like he's happy you're there, but not completely sure who let you in. You drop the subject.

But it's not just the conference room. The premise of this series seems, well—*slight*. Two good-looking, divorced people meet and decide to—date! Not exactly groundbreaking. You watch *The Sopranos*, your heart sinking. You've got concerns. You've got this musical you're supposed to be writing. You meet the director that Marshall and Ed just hired and take an instant dislike to him. It's mutual. You meet the actors. You have no idea what to say to them and that's mutual, too. Actually, there's nothing to say to anyone because now you're in production, where talk is worse than

---

cheap, it's unshootable. There's nothing to do but write.

Doing a series raises questions—well, one question really, over and over: *Will there be enough?* Enough time. Enough story. Enough approval. This is actually a trick question and you know that, but for a while you let it rule your life. Your mind becomes a too-small conference room filled with actors you can't please, phone calls you can't return, conversations with your husband that you'll never, ever get to finish because you're locked in a very small room with a very small premise, *writing*.

Once in a while, on the set, eating food you shouldn't be eating, or on the long drive home, it hits you—you have no idea who these characters *are!* You decide to pretend you do. You decide to make the characters confused; you give them your own confusion, which makes sense. (Or you decide to pretend it does.) You notice with amazement (even though it's happened to you many times before) that everything you decide to pretend about the characters instantly becomes *who they are*. Like a magic spell! You love this. You decide to bring in more characters, to keep the characters you never understood in the first place company. The conference room gets even more crowded: The schizophrenic brother. The P.J. Harvey fan. The visionary cappuccino repairman. You write an episode involving the main character's father and when Paul Mazursky reads it out loud, your own, no-longer-living father is suddenly there, with you, in the crowded conference room.

You're still on the air. The two divorced people aren't dating anymore. They aren't even two divorced people anymore. They're you. And Marshall. And Ed. And every other writer on the show. You want to tell Ed and Marshall how much all of this means to you, but you can't find the words, and the meeting's almost over. There's nothing to do but finish the script, break another story and realize the instant dislike between you and that director is actually a precious friendship. So you wander down to the set to find him, and actors take you aside and tell you things you didn't know you needed. Not only actors. Wardrobe people, prop people. All people. Your every encounter becomes just what you needed. You use things your daughter says, things your therapist says— wherever you go, there's the line you need. Ideas tap you on the shoulder at Starbucks and follow you home.

You feel the end drawing near. Everyone does. You thank the craft service guy for all the delicious food, and go upstairs for the last table read of the last episode of the series. You look around the room. The actors. The other writers. Marshall and Ed. You love them. You love them so much that there's absolutely nothing to say. You sit and listen as the last script is read, realizing—you don't need more space, or higher ratings, or one more season. As it turns out, there was plenty of time. The room was just the right size.

# Terry Rossio

## On Location

---

*"It has our favorite line of the movie—and we take full credit."*

Terry Rossio prefers to work in a writing team, to split the rewards and distribute the blame. With writing partner Ted Elliott, Rossio co-wrote the animated film *Aladdin*; also the live-action films *The Mask of Zorro* and *Pirates of the Caribbean*, as well as the animated feature *Shrek*, for which the pair received an Academy Award® nomination.

Our favorite line we wrote for *Pirates of the Caribbean* is one we didn't write.

This is how it goes, some days, when you're a writer working on the set of a major motion picture:

6:15 a.m., my writing partner, Ted Elliott, and I got called into Gore Verbinski's office after a 30-minute morning commute to work via ferry along the coast of St. Vincent (yeah, sure beats the 405 at rush hour). Gore explained there was a change planned for that day's shooting. The stunt guys had figured out a brilliant way to pull Johnny Depp out of the water onto the moving ship—but it meant Depp had to land back near the ship's wheel. The script

---

had called for him to land midships and move toward the wheel. The new staging meant Depp's character had to say something to order his crew away and leave him alone for the final shot—

And since this was the end shot of the movie, could we come up with a command that was interesting, meaningful, a bit more profound than "Back to work, mates!"

Sure. Ted went off to talk to the Captain of one of the film's working ships, the *Lady Washington*, and try to scare up some authentic nautical commands. I went to find Depp and warn him that some new dialogue was coming. Johnny was cool with it and even had suggestions—as research for the role, he'd been reading stories of seafaring men, he said, so, "How about something like, 'We venture forth over waves of adversity beneath clouds of adventure, always searching for the elusive shore of our dreams..'?"

"Right," I said... "Uh, something just like that. We're working on it."

So I go hook up with Ted on the *Lady Washington*, and they've come up with some possible phrases. There were a few that weren't right at all—chief among them, I recall, was "Put the wind to our aft!" That's just not a line you want as the last line of your movie. We all liked the phrase, "Let go, and haul to run free!" I particularly liked that "run free" seemed appropriate to Depp's character, who considered his ship to be a symbol of freedom.

So we find Gore and run that line past him, he wrinkles his nose, says, "I dunno, I get kind of a *Born Free* vibe out of that. Maybe something else?"

So it's back to the *Lady Washington*. We get a call that Depp wants us to meet him in makeup, but the ship is on the way, so we stop off there first to try to come up with a better line.

Now I will always remember this:

We hear a shout, look over, and there's Johnny Depp racing toward us full speed from the trailers, only half in costume, waving a piece of paper over his head. He's shouting—I kid you not— "I've got it! Got it!"

He races full speed toward the gangplank, and let me tell you something about gangplanks, they're not very sturdy. Whenever we went across, the production was careful to have two sailors present, on either end, to help you on and off. Depp wasn't waiting for that—he bounded onto the gangplank, it bounced him up into the air, and light as a feather he comes down on it, bounces up again, and lands gracefully on deck. Hey, that's why he gets the big bucks. So he comes up to us, a little out of breath and says, "I got it," and shows us the paper.

Well, with a buildup like that, and from your major star, you'd better hope that the line is good. Ted and I look at the paper, and, beneath a bunch of crossed-off efforts, Depp wrote—

"Bring me that horizon!"

Ted and I look at each other.

"That's pretty good," Ted says.

"Yeah," I said. "Really good."

Hell, it was fantastic. We put it together with the other line and it sounded great, "Let go and haul to run free! Bring me that horizon!"

We took it to Gore. He listened, thought about it for all of half a second, said, "That's pretty good. That's really good. Hell, it's fantastic." Now he even liked the "run free" lead-in, too.

So by midmorning we were rehearsing the scene. The only thing left was the first line, the reference to the crew. Depp gamely tried to act our first effort, which I think was, "What are you looking at, you ricket-ridden layabouts! Back to work!" After spitting that out a few times, he simply demanded something else. We worked through a few—Depp's candidate was "starving maggots," but I pointed out that seemed like a contradiction—and then Ted came up with "Scabrous dogs."

So, the end line of the movie was finally set:

JACK SPARROW
What are you lookin' at, you scabrous dogs?
Back to work! Let go and haul to run free!
Bring me that horizon!

As of this writing, I don't know if the movie is good, or if the lines made it in, or even if they work the way they should. But if the film is good, it's fun to think that the final line of the film was written the day it was shot.

I hope it does work.

I hope the movie is great. I hope it's a classic.

Because I've got something pinned above my desk. The scrap of paper Depp was waving as he raced out of the trailer, the one he wrote the line on—

I kept it, of course. It has our favorite line of the movie—and we take full credit.

# John Sacret Young

## The Actor with the Coffee Can

---

*"Credence was the issue."*  John Sacret Young co-created and executive produced the Emmy® Award-winning *China Beach* and wrote the feature films *Testament* and *Romero*. He has won the WGA Award, the Humanitas Prize and the Christopher Award twice each, as well as a Golden Globe and a Peabody Award.

He was just an actor carrying a coffee can.

He was a carpenter as well as an actor with a coffee can it turned out, and that was how he was making his living then.

He was hired to play a high school biology teacher. It was $3,000 for a week's work and he didn't fly.

He arrived in Portland, Oregon, and at Reed College by bus for the shooting of my first pilot, a 90-minute one—an unusual length then and unheard of now. He had his coffee can and notes, under his arm, thicker than the script.

The producer, a man prone to a richness of enthusiasm and riotous overstatement, called me even before the actor with the coffee can was hired. "There's this guy in my office. He's great, he's

---

sexy, he's perfect for the part," he said, "and he's going to be a star. You've got to come down right now and meet him."

I was still falling off the turnip truck and occupying a cramped and abandoned cranny with fake pine-panel walls and cottage-cheese ceilings as black around the air-conditioning ducts as the inside of an old fireplace. And where I came from, you don't drop everything to meet "a sexy guy," no matter how perfect.

I was to learn the producer said such things. He said such things about people I've never heard of since. He was an extraordinary creature and a great champion. He also thought screaming was whispering and arguing was breathing. The plague of AIDS wiped him out.

The director was the son of a director who never mentioned his father. At age 29, he had headed a studio and produced a violent and remarkable television series. For actors, it was a steppingstone into movies. Twenty-some years later, the series itself steppingstoned into an Oscar® -winning movie.

The studio refused to pay for a writer to go on location. It would set or break precedent; I was never sure which or why. The producer and director split my plane ticket, I paid for my meals, and I camped on the couch in the living room of the producer's suite.

The hotel had never seen good days and was well into bad ones. The shag rug in the suite was the color of Trix cereal. Pink, yellow, and orange. At night, I could hear—or witness if I chose to look—the mice slaloming through the shag.

The director called together a table read. He prided himself on his cool and his control, but quickly questions came my way—the script had a certain cadence and I had a certain quality—and

quickly I was sent away—banished wouldn't be the wrong word—
to do rewrites.

I wasn't in the rubber room long before the phone rang. It was
the director and he wasn't cool and controlled. His voice was an
urgent and hissing whisper: "I told everybody not to hire this guy.
He's killing me. You're going to have to come down here right
now." Before I could, the phone rang again. It was the first AD.
The director couldn't wait, he said, he's sending the actor and his
coffee can up to you.

So the actor-with-his-coffee-can-who-was-a-killer-and-going-to-
be-a-star knocked and came in and sat down in the only other chair.

He was lean and intense and had a scar on his chin. His
features were outsized and imperfect yet memorable. His hair was
full and wiry and his hands were tough and callused from his
carpentry.

I was to learn he had completed two movies. They were in the
can and had been a long time—they were talked about sometimes
hopefully, sometimes mockingly; no one knew what would happen
to them—and he was broke.

I was to learn both movies would be remarkable and
groundbreaking.

I was to learn he lived down the street from me on the corner
of Woodrow Wilson Drive in the Hollywood Hills.

I was to learn many things when he would come up and sit in
my kitchen overlooking the canyon and smoke a joint or two.

But that was later.

In the room, he set the coffee can on the shag rug and

unshuffled his notes. He had questions about his role—he had a lot of questions. They were well thought out. He was very literal and very serious and he was testing himself—the role and the reasons why he was doing it—and me. Me as me, and me as a stand-in for the once cool and controlled and now-absent director.

Credence was the issue. He wanted it and wanted to know if I had it.

It wasn't so long before I ran out of truth and bullshit about the character, this biology teacher who was smart and savvy and had a secret: he was having an affair with a student.

We reached that point where I said I'll look at anything but this is the way I wrote him and why.

The actor looked at me and put down his wad of notes, all of them. "Okay, that's done," he said. We had passed some kind of test. "You'll look and you'll do what you're going to do. But there's one scene and there's no choice about this one. I've got an idea that will make it so much better."

The scene was a crucial one. In it, the biology teacher tempts a class of girls to come up and unscrew the top of a glass jar and reach a hand in. The jar has a spider in it, big, black and thready-looking.

Finally, one skittish and scared girl approaches the jar. The spider appears huge through the distorting glass. Timidly, she touches the top, starts to unscrew it. The teacher makes a sound and she jumps a foot and scampers back toward her seat. The class howls. The teacher pulls the spider out and there's a reason it looks thready.

That's what it is. Thread, black thread, black thread tangled into the shape of a spider.

That's his point: know what you're scared of and why; don't base it on superstition. Most spiders do good, few are poisonous.

The actor felt the scene was "bogus," it wasn't real, and he had the solution. He picked up his coffee can and took its top off and turned the can upside down and shook it.

An item proceeded to plop onto the shag rug. A large and hairy item. A large and hairy item that sprung around the pink and the yellow and the orange.

A large and hairy tarantula item.

The actor with the coffee can had done his homework, been creative, used his initiative, and he was pleased.

I managed somehow to stay in my chair and learned an essential lesson: I was going to have to convince this strong, intelligent, bus-riding star-to-be to see that this jumping item would legitimately terrify anybody and would completely upend and reverse the intended meaning of the scene.

Or there would be no credence between us.

The actor with the coffee can and I watched the tarantula jump around the room for a long time.

The thread stayed in the scene, the actor with the coffee can went on to become Harrison Ford—and I don't know what happened to the tarantula.

# Wesley Strick

## The Snit

---

*"The Star has read the Writer's draft and has 'a few ideas.'"*

Wesley Strick has written, co-written, directed or written and directed ten films (okay, one was for cable) including *Cape Fear*, *Doom* and *Arachnophobia*. He has rewritten an equal number, uncredited. His uncredited films have all been bigger hits than his credited films, proving that the Movie Gods love irony as much as any screenwriter.

The Writer flies to London to hook up with the Director, a big, bluff, lovable (is there any other kind?) Aussie. Together, the two catch a plane for Johannesburg (the Writer's second 11-hour flight in two days). At Jo'burg, they board a prop plane no bigger than a station wagon with wings, and fly into the bush, landing on a runway (read: dirt road) adjacent to a resort called Badplaas (read: bad place). Why have they come all this way?

To meet with the Star, of course, who's completing work on a period film set in Africa and has installed himself in a magnificent tent in the middle of a nature reserve. The Star has read the Writer's draft and has "a few ideas."

---

But first he barks at the Writer: "What are the essential qualities of my Character's personality?" The profoundly jet-lagged Writer (who has not met the Star before, but has been warned that the Star is legendarily difficult) stammers out a short list. When he's done, the Star observes, "Nothing you just said makes me feel any better about playing this part."

It turns out that the Star doesn't like this sort of movie (action/thriller). In fact, he clarifies, "I don't like movies." The Writer glances at the Director—this could be a problem. All three men know that, even now, mammoth sets are being built at Pinewood in anticipation of a shoot to begin two months hence. Star, Director and Writer sit around a campfire that the Star's assistant has built. The Writer is trying to stay both warm and sane by gulping large quantities of Scotch that the Star has graciously offered.

It is the only gracious offering that the Star will ever make to the Writer.

Many hours have elapsed. The Star is engaged in a marathon monologue, a sometimes-surreal stream of consciousness, in which he imagines his character in a variety of situations existential and suspenseful, none of which have any bearing on the script that is being prepped in England, and all of which violate every principle of movie storytelling that the Writer has ever learned.

The Writer suspects the sun is about to come up. He doesn't wish to be awake and still hearing the Star's "notes" when this happens; he says he needs sleep. The Star, though miffed, agrees that the meeting may continue tomorrow. The Writer and Director stumble off to their tent, some hundred yards away. As soon as they've closed the flaps, the Director confides, "I know you want to walk off the picture, mate. But if you leave now, you'll be eaten by tigers." Because of this jest, the Writer decides to stick it out.

Months later, midway through production, the Star calls a story meeting one Sunday morning at the London hotel where Director and Writer are staying.

He is anxious to know why a particular scene he'd demanded has never appeared in any version of the script. The scene's premise is impossible, nearly insane. The Writer earnestly explains, "I've tried several times to write the scene, but I just can't make sense of it." Turning deep red, the Star shouts, "Just because you can't make sense of it doesn't mean I can't act it."

The Writer's family wants him to come home. His two young sons are in a grade school talent show the day after tomorrow. Rueful, the Writer explains that a key scene is coming up, on which the Star has still not signed off. It's imperative that the Writer be on set, ready to make last-minute revisions.

On the morning the scene is to be shot, the Director summons the Writer to his trailer and sheepishly explains that the Star and his Leading Lady have rewritten the scene themselves. They've asked that the Writer not be present when they're shooting, lest they feel self-conscious. The Writer nods.

But the Writer's bloodstream seethes with adrenaline. He walks back from the Soho location to his hotel, where he packs his bags and (making a point of not telling anyone on the production) checks out, cabs to Heathrow and flies home to Los Angeles. The bad news is, he's missed the talent show.

The good news is, he's free.

A year later, at the premiere, the Writer finds himself standing beside the Producer at—where else?—the bar. The Producer says, "I still don't get why you quit the movie." The Writer shrugs, then orders another Cosmo.

Some things, you can't explain.

# Leslie Dixon

## Dish Served Cold

---

*"Never believe a writer's tale of woe, 'Oh, my brilliant script was ruined.'"*

Leslie Dixon spent ten years as a comedy writer (*Mrs. Doubtfire, Overboard, Outrageous Fortune*) before realizing that respect for screenwriters only accrues in direct proportion to pretentiousness. She then turned her back on comedy, trying new genres with *The Thomas Crown Affair* and *Pay It Forward*. After her experiences on the latter, her goal is to write silent films.

In 2000, I had one of my better scripts fatally mangled. Why? Well—let's take a political pause and think. Should I be venal? Fingerpoint? Assign blame? Twist my arm: it was all the actors' fault.

SIDE NOTE: Never believe a writer's tale of woe, "Oh, my brilliant script was ruined." They will proceed to tell you, "*My* version of the scene where she regained her sight was so much better." There can be, sometimes, not the dimmest awareness that the film was a turd from the get-go.

That said, there are barometers by which writers can judge if their script was ever any good. If you get 50 job offers after your agent circulates the material, if big stars are clamoring to do it, that's a pretty fair indication you've delivered. By those standards, at least, *Pay It Forward* was a success.

I was coming off *The Thomas Crown Affair*. Ooh. Let's talk about those actors for a minute.

Here's Pierce Brosnan: we're having a script meeting in a hip London hotel lounge. Across the room are two girls having a drink. They're young—barely 21 and all dressed up—it looks like one of them was buying the other a birthday drink at a "posh" place—thrilled just to be there. They are sneaking looks at Pierce, awed to be across the room from him, but desperately wanting to be classy. They weren't going to go over and bother him. It was enough just to be breathing the same air.

Pierce saw them, took it all in. Next thing the girls knew, a waiter appeared at their side. "Mr. Brosnan would like to send you both a drink." It was fun watching them try not to faint. He raised his glass to them, wanting nothing—*certainly* not a sleazy pickup, just deriving pleasure from their stammering thanks.

It must be nice, with a simple gesture, to be able to give people something to tell their grandchildren.

Here's Rene Russo: It's the premiere of *Thomas Crown*. I arrive behind her. She's already on the red carpet, in front of the paparazzi. They're snapping away. She sees me, grabs me, clamps an arm around me so I can't get away and says, "This is the writer! I wouldn't be here tonight if it wasn't for her wonderful script!" She doesn't let go of me, forcing them to take *my* picture if they're going to get anything of her. Grudgingly, they continue to snap.

The movie gods, watching all this, must have decided to cast me out of heaven, down, into one of Dante's inner circles.

I hadn't exactly heard warm, fuzzy things about Kevin Spacey and Helen Hunt. He was supposed to be tough, and she currently held, by rumor, the title of Most Difficult Working Actress.

At least they were great actors, which was lucky, because *Pay It Forward* was an easy film to ruin. It was about a burned out, cynical teacher who gives his class an assignment to come up with an idea that will change the world. He doesn't believe for a minute that the kids are capable of such a thing, it's just a rote assignment that always produces predictably lazy results. When one 7th grader takes the assignment seriously, the teacher is profoundly affected.

The tone of the movie needed to be *Tender Mercies*. Not faux Capra. The characters needed to be matter-of-fact, inarticulate, to cut the treacle of that dreaded trap—moral uplift.

Helen was actually quite charming until the first moment I politely disagreed with her. Her mouth set, her eyes grew hard, and I don't recall that she ever again demonstrated the slightest pretense of civility. I quickly learned that anyone who said anything but Yes to her was, then and forever, the enemy.

Immediately, Kevin let me know my caste. During our first meeting, he began making phone calls in front of me, without ever saying "Excuse me," or acknowledging that a person was sitting there, waiting. I was wallpaper.

Finally off the phone, he announced that he wanted a change in his character: "I think he should be a *good* teacher and really connect with those kids."

My heart sank. I did *not* say, "Um, Inspirational Teacher 101 is a moldy movie formula from the dawn of sound!" Instead I mentioned, gingerly, that moral transformations did seem to be more powerful when they happen to cynical people.

Well, but he'd played a lot of cynical people. He wanted to be cuddly.

He also wanted a lot more on-screen backstory about how his character had been physically scarred by his father. He did not come out and say the words, "Give me a big, scenery-chewing speech," but I got the message. More paragraphs. Can't win the Oscar® without talking a lot!

Helen's first of many demands was that she be seen not as a tenuously recovered alcoholic but still fighting the demons of the bottle. Again, I was distraught—oh dear, *drunk* scenes. Territory covered by so many actresses in so many movies. She'd be staggering, wallowing, throwing up.

One morning, she took me aside. "I was talking to my therapist about this character, and she said, well, the way this woman behaves, she's a classic case of a person molested as a child."

"Oh," I said, wary.

"And it's *very* important to me that this be made clear."

"That she was molested as a child."

"Yes."

"On camera. In dialogue."

"Yes."

"You do realize… that this would make dueling child-abuse backstories for you and Kevin."

It didn't matter. She wanted her very own underage grope, and she was going to get it.

I stared at the producer and director. No one said boo.

Resigned, I began making the script worse. There weren't wrenching changes; it was more the death by a thousand little razor cuts. A few things got better... when I saw that the delightful Haley Joel Osment was not the dour little thing of *Sixth Sense*, but in fact a light spirit, I wrote more humor for him, which improved his scenes.

The week before production I spent in Las Vegas, separated from my family, in a windowless conference room, for what were supposedly rehearsals. In fact, it was simply, in Helen's own words, a "script autopsy," days spent picking at, criticizing, and reshaping the thing down to the last comma. No word was too small to escape protracted and negative discussion. (Kevin once gave a 45-minute soliloquy, the end result of which was that he wanted one line changed.) Occasionally, I was yelled at—more often, just ignored. A week passed in which no one said a personal word to me; even knee-jerk courtesies like "Hello" and "Goodbye" had gone by the wayside.

"What's it like?" my agent asked, on the phone.

"Like being trapped in a cell with Mengele and Eichmann."

I wondered, if they thought so little of me, why didn't they ask for another writer? But the days passed and it didn't happen. No–no–don't tell me—*I wasn't going to be fired*—! Could a room be that cold, that free of nutrients, like an airlock, and *not* portend a firing?

Apparently, it could.

No longer consoled by the certainty that the end was near, I began to crack. As I was sniveling to my husband one night on the phone, he pointed out that I alone, out of everyone on that movie, could, within 48 hours, be floating down the Grand Canal in a gondola.

I quit.

Time passed; I finally saw the film. Everything I dreaded had happened: looming closeups, ham-fisted dialogue, searing obviousness, a jarring ending. My agent asked me, "How was it?" "Not my kind of movie," I said, wishing I'd written *Reservoir Dogs*.

Annoyed at my desertion, the actors began taking pot shots at the script. It had been "goo," they said during their publicity junket, but they had gotten in there, rolled up their sleeves, made it ring of Truth.

The critics disagreed.

I lay low, licked my wounds. But when my *mother* called, after reading a movie magazine, and said, "Well! Those actors certainly don't think much of *you*, do they?," something in me began to boil. Was I really going to lie down for that?—Well, if I wanted to remain a professional screenwriter, I should; I should *bend* over for that. Besides, wasn't I a classy person? Too mature and spiritually evolved for petty vengeance?

Soon after, a *Wall Street Journal* reporter began poking around, curious as to why this film, released with the studio's highest expectations, had flopped. He quickly determined that the actors had been calling the shots from day one. In the ensuing article, he made the observation that perhaps Mr. Spacey's judgment about corniness wasn't entirely to be trusted, since this was the man who improvised, on camera:

> EUGENE (KEVIN SPACEY)
> I don't want to spend another
> second of wasted air, you beautiful,
> lovely, difficult hilarious woman.
> Please don't let me stay trapped in here
> forever. I'm so exhausted from being
> so afraid.

Phones rang. The Powers That Be were raging. That speech was cut from the film! How the hell could that reporter have seen it?

Oops. Well. I guess *someone* gave him the shooting script.

As if in apology, the movie gods next threw me Steve Martin. I wrote my brains out for him, turned it in. He called the next day. Just wanted to say how pleased he was.

# SECRETS OF THE HOLLYWOOD PROS #5:

## Hitting the Right Note

To screenwriters, "note" is a four-letter word.

But if we believe, as most of us do, that writing is rewriting, then we must also believe that a good script note—one which correctly apprehends our intentions, incisively illuminates where we have gone wrong and guides us back onto the path to realizing the promise of our work—is to be welcomed like a St. Bernard after an avalanche. But, hey, let's get back to the real world and the kind of notes you too often get in Hollywood, which are given in the spirit of the old joke: "Why does a dog lick his balls? Because he can."

When you work, you will get notes. And because your work is owned by someone else—whether it is a so-called "work for hire," aka an assignment, or an original screenplay that you've sold to a studio or production company—you can either deal with the notes or know that they will hire someone who will. That's why knowing how to deal with notes is an essential survival skill.

Recently, film, television and stage writer Shelly Goldstein compiled and edited interviews with several writers for the Writers Guild of America. John Boni, whose credits include

*Three's Company, Facts of Life*, the cult classic *Fernwood 2Nite* and the *Robin Hood* spoof *When Things Were Rotten*, which he co-created with Mel Brooks, offers some great practical tips for dealing with the process of getting notes. In his bio, John claims to be a very good dancer. I wouldn't know about that, but I did work with him on 227 and can personally attest that he can both give and receive a good note. On second thought, I do recall him skillfully dancing around a network note or two. So, without further ado, here's John Boni:

The inescapable reality is that when a writer sells something, the person who paid him owns it. He, or one, two or five of his minions have the keys to the note floodgates. The writer can either swim with the flow and deal with them or, if contractually possible, yank away the script in a creative snit. The latter choice is extreme and nonproductive, the former is merely distasteful. The trick is to try to make the distasteful choice more appetizing.

I believe that dealing with notes is a practical problem, not an artistic one. Knowing how to take a note is an essential survival skill, if only because the producer has the mother of all trump cards: If you don't execute his notes, he'll find another writer who will.

The object is to negotiate, not to fight or win. The object is to get the movie made. The object is to live to write more scripts that get made. The object is to establish your reputation as a writer one can work with so you'll be hired to write other scripts that get made. Finally, none of us is Shakespeare. What we're called upon to write will hardly be categorized as immortal. What we should strive for is a piece that is original, entertaining, professional and well-crafted, something you can be proud of. Having said that, let's get to some practical techniques to help the writer handle a producer's bad notes. I'm assuming the following:

1. As much as can be determined, your script generally makes sense.

2. The producer is not an asshole and can be reasoned with.

If he's a stubborn idiot, God save us all. So, just extrapolate from the following what you can use.

A quick aside. I HATE the use of "he or she," "his or her" as generic pronouns, or as the grammarians call them, the epicine pronouns. Here is an area where political correctness has contaminated the language and made it clunky. My personal solution is for a man—that's me—to use the masculine pronouns when referring to a generic person and for a woman writer to use the feminine pronouns. So, I will be using "he," "his" and "him" throughout, knowing full well that many producers and executives are female.

Back to the notes.

Remember always that this is a very subjective business. Be as objective as you can in determining whether a producer's notes will really sink the script. Ask yourself honestly if you're being stubborn or egotistical about your work. Or proprietary! Do you believe that only your approach is the right one? Are you the kind of writer who is generally open to other points of view?

These are hard questions of self-examination, but they nevertheless need honest thought. I recommend you ask them before going ballistic over the producer's requests.

Next, divide the producer's notes into major and minor. Though some could overlap, major notes are those that mess with the story, the mechanics of the plot, change characterizations, involve scene restructuring or substantial scene cutting, additions and resequencing. These are notes that represent vertical changes in your script.

Minor notes are line changes, name changes, scene trimming or lengthening, minor character changes, changes in locations, alternate jokes or gags and so on. These are lateral changes. They often don't affect the structure or integrity of the script, but they do make a difference. My advice is to give the producer these lateral changes. Just give them to him. Let him win. How critical is it to the script's integrity if the producer wants a scene set in a park on a sunny day but you're in love with the scene as you wrote it with the two characters charmingly dodging the rain in city traffic? Not much, so let the sun shine in. By conceding these changes, you're parlaying your own reasonableness and goodwill into a personal equity that will help you fight the notes that will cause major damage to your script—the dreaded vertical changes.

Incidentally, some lateral changes can be ignored. As the writer, you should be able to justify every word on the page. The producer, however, is just "reacting" to stuff, and like all of us, he'll often react differently to the same thing on different days. So figure the notegiver will forget many of these lateral suggestions because they were probably reactive ones, ephemeral notions that occurred to him that day because his shoes were too tight or he was in a great or bad mood. Chances are you can give him the rewrite without those particular changes. If he does remember some of them, slap your forehead and say you missed that one. Sorry! I'll catch it on the next draft—and there *will* be a next draft, and a next and a next.

Vertical changes can significantly improve or damage a script. They're difference makers. They affect outcomes. A good vertical note can transform a script and a writer should be alert to them. The bad ones are like jury tampering, but without recourse to a judge or the police. They might mess with the mechanics of the plot so that the story doesn't make sense. They might change the characters in such a way that *they* don't make sense. If so, some carefully thought-out rebuttals might illustrate the error of his suggestions, i.e., "but Mr. Producer, if we have our protagonist do *Action A* then it doesn't follow that he would do *Action B* 20 scenes later."

In a workmanlike manner, take each vertical change to its logical script extension and demonstrate the distortions that the change would cause. Often, producers become enamored of an idea without understanding its script repercussions. They don't think like writers, who actively calculate on the spot how each change will affect the creative house of cards that is your story. Producers are just enamored of the change, even if it's one of the foundation cards. Chances are they're not even aware that it's a foundation card. Sometimes just clearly pointing out the ripple effect of the change can cause him to abandon it.

It's always a plus if you can show how his change will ripple effect some of his favorite parts of the film. If he really loves *Action B* and you show him how his *Action A* change will eliminate *Action B*, you've painted him into a creative corner. Now *he's* the one who has to face the tough choice. Facing tough choices makes us all vulnerable. It's a good time to win a point.

My feeling is that most of these people think they're writers or want to be writers, but haven't the patience or the courage to try it. Pay them the compliment of dealing with them as a co-writer, a fellow craftsman. Speak to them as if they're familiar with the process. The note discussion will then be occurring between two writers, not between producer/power guy and writer/defenseless guy. "Well, you know this kind of scene usually doesn't write well" or "from a writing point of view, you can see how this might not work," wink, wink, nudge nudge. Including them is flattering and puts them on insecure ground because they only know producer stuff, not writer stuff. But here you are, inviting one of them into the writer's process. It's hard to feel sure of yourself when you're operating in unknown territory. In a deft about-face, you can throw in something like, "As a *producer*, you know you can show that dramatically" etc.

Some of this is your own bullshit, but what the hell, it's a bullshit business.

Most important, whatever your objection or agreement, always explain why. Don't offer feelings or vagueries. Have a *story* reason for everything you want or don't want to change. Where possible, cite other films that support your responses.

Another trick is to put the producer on the defensive by being very positive. "I want to make this character a dwarf," says the producer. Your eyes light up. "A fun idea," you say, "but how do we handle the basketball sequence and his joining the army, with its height requirement, where he heroically fends off a rogue SWAT team at the end?" Uhhhhhh...

Though an exaggerated example, the point is, wherever you can, let the producer feel the pain of figuring out the impossible residue of his note. Don't do it challengingly. Make him believe that your enquiring mind really wants to know. Maybe when he has to stew in the residual morass of his suggestion, he'll come to realize how bad it is and you can chalk up another win. At the least, just because he's the producer doesn't mean you can't make him suffer a little.

However, at script impasses like this, the crafty producer will say something like, "Hey, you're the writer. I leave that to you."

This is an anthrax cocktail and don't ever leave with him leaving it up to you. Don't blink, don't cave. Immediately try to come up with some suggestions on the spot—all in the spirit of collaborating. Let him know you're speaking off the top of your head and work with him as you spitball where this damn script is headed. Always try to pin him down to an approach on the major changes before you leave for the rewrite struggle. Tell him your "collegial" insistence on finding solutions is only because you want to make sure he likes what he's going to get. Otherwise, your rewrite might contain choices he'll hate, and the chances are that he *will* hate them because, truly, his notes and the subsequent adjustments might not track as well as you'd all like. He'll see it in the black and white of the rewrite, but will never blame his original note for it. You'll get the blame. Hey, you're the writer, remember!? So it's important to protect your butt and try to come to some agreement on how to change the subsequent scenes that his original note(s) generated. He'll be more likely to approve the rewrite if he's been a co-conspirator on the changes.

Spitballing in his presence could also get him to agree to a particular approach. If he does, make a show of writing it down carefully and getting him to acknowledge he's a co-conspirator in this plot change. If it goes south, you can be as disappointed as he is when you tell him, "Gee, you liked the idea as much as I did when we discussed it."

I repeat, it's all subjective. You can't *prove* your way is better. There are no stats in this game. You can't show that your script hit .320 and his version hit .285. You will not win without his cooperation and collaboration. Get him on your side and let him feel he had a creative stake in the outcome.

The key is preparation. The famous legal dictum, "Don't ask a question you don't know the answer to," can be helpful.

"Don't give him an alternative you're not certain about." This is easier to do if he types out the notes and sends them to you before your meeting—preferred, and ask for that. If he gives his notes in person, try not to do battle then and there. Write down the notes, ask to think about them and come back for the "prepared" session. If that's not possible, use as many of the above techniques as you can under the circumstances.

Whether he knows it or not, whether you know it or not, this is best approached as a negotiation, not as a creative free-for-all.

Finally, when all is said and done, writing is a craft. With your back to the script-sinking rewrite wall, call upon all your powers to craft the best possible script within the limits the producer has created. Don't give up. Don't sulk. Make it something worthwhile in spite of him. Use the opportunity to exercise your creative muscles rather than bitch about his stupidities.

Remember the charming scene in the rain that you wrote for those two characters? Now that the producer wants it in the park in the sun, figure a way to make *that* scene as charming. You don't have the rain, but you have the sun, the hot day, perhaps roller-bladers interrupting their talk, a nurse with a baby, some buskers juggling nearby—put the same inventiveness into the change that you put into the original. That's the craft of this process and it's really all we have. We're trying to do the best job we can, with as much insight and creativity as we can muster, and often that lies as much in the craft as it does in the original vision. Do your best and beat the bastards at their own game.

After John Boni's practicum on "Notes: Can't Ignore Them—Can't Shove Them Up The Note-Givers Old Wazoo," the last word goes to Ian Abrams, who wrote the feature *Undercover Blues* and created the CBS series *Early Edition*. Ian, also speaking in Shelly Goldstein's *Written By* piece, illuminates the spirit in which you should take all notes.

"My brother Aron, wise beyond his years, once told me when I was grousing about the latest atrocity I was performing at an exec's command, 'In Florida, they use illegal Haitian immigrants to harvest sugar cane. They work in the sun in 110-degree heat, ten hours at a time stooping over harvesting the cane, making a miserable few bucks a day—and they don't have creative control, either.'"

*"Anybody can become a writer, but the trick is to STAY a writer."*

—Harlan Ellison

# Chapter 6

## In a clearing stands a boxer:[6]

## Surviving The Course

---

Several years ago, Frank Pierson and a bunch of film students saved me from drowning.

WARNING: EDITOR'S PERSONAL REMEMBRANCE AHEAD!

Rather than write yet another dazzlingly brilliant but impersonal lead to the next essays, your editor has succumbed to the urge to share his own experiences. If you don't want to share, then, by all means, continue on to our next essays, which examine the Hollywood laws of physics: a) what goes up must come down, and b) for the lucky and the brave, what comes down sometimes may also go back up.

So, as I was saying to you...

Several years ago, Frank Pierson and a bunch of film students saved me from drowning.

6. From *The Boxer* © Paul Simon

---

They call it swimming with sharks; but my attitude was "Come on in, the water's fine!" I was a survivor. A dozen years as a working writer in Hollywood. Got upended by the tsunami known as the Writers' Guild Strike of 1988; but within a year, I was in the curl again: co-wrote a Number-One movie; earned an Emmy® nomination and a Humanitas Prize nomination. At the power table of a trendy Hollywood eatery where even the staff wore all black, my agent had leaned over a salad as studiedly arranged as a Bel-Air lawn, and said to me, "A lot of people in this town want to be in the Daryl Nickens business." Oh, yes. Somewhere in the eternal sunshine of my ego, I was young Robert Evans poised on the diving board of the pool at the Beverly Hills Hotel, all eyes on me....

And then my career did a huge belly flop. Who knows why? Was it saying "Yes" when I should have said "No?" Or "No" when I should have said "Yes?" Was it not listening to my agent (the savant)? Or was it listening to my agent (the idiot)? Was it what I wrote? Or was it what I didn't write? All I know is, I had emerged from the pool a middle-aged black writer, which is to say, unemployable. Worst of all, I was active in the Writers Guild, which started to seem like a particularly sadistic form of self-abuse because I was working on behalf of working writers; that is, writers currently making money from writing, which increasingly I wasn't.

One day at a meeting of the Writers Guild's Committee on Committees (which sounds like a relative of Firesign Theatre's Department of Redundancy Department), I happened to ask fellow member Frank Pierson how he had approached the adaptation of a novel I knew he was doing because a writing partner, Deborah Baron, and I happened to have been up for the assignment to adapt the same book. Not surprisingly, Frank, the multiple Academy Award® winner, got the job. On the surface, the book seemed cinematic enough: a thriller, with plenty of plot and action from an author of an earlier novel, that had been turned into one of the great films of the '70s; but underneath, because the what-is-this-really-about? thematic connective tissue seemed weak, it was tough to see exactly where the movie was emotionally. So I had genuine intellectual curiosity when I asked Frank how the adaptation was going. To my surprise, he said that he wasn't sure that he had cracked it. Would I mind reading his draft and giving him some notes?

It took every ounce of self-control I possessed not to sputter the biggest Jackie Gleason "Huhminah-huhminah!" since the Great One said it in his heyday. I managed to shrug, "Sure, I could do that…"

When Frank's script arrived in the mail, I remembered something I had learned the hard way from a brief experience as a sparring partner for the Kickboxing Federation's World Heavyweight Champion: you don't play a casual round of golf with Tiger Woods; you don't shoot a fun game of H-O-R-S-E with Michael Jordan; and you don't just dash off a couple of notes to Frank Pierson. I spent several days reading and rereading his script. I spent several more thinking and rethinking, writing and rewriting my notes. Finally, I sent them off, hoping I hadn't thoroughly embarrassed myself, though I felt I was poised on that diving board again: fat, black and naked.

Two days later, Frank left a message on my answering machine, thanking me for the best notes he had ever gotten in his 40 years in Hollywood. In case you think I'm exaggerating, I can play the tape for you, which I'm not too proud to say I saved.

When we talked, Frank, who among his dizzying array of

activities in addition to his own career, was Chair of the AFI Conservatory, asked if I would be interested in helping out with a project over there.

Several weeks later, I was supervising script development for all First Year films at AFI. I met with each writer/director/producer team. I heard pitches. Gave notes. Read scripts. Gave more notes. Read revisions; gave even more notes. I conducted final-draft meetings with the entire production team. And, of course, gave still more notes. I helped bring 75 little movies into the world. I worked with gifted students like Patty Jenkins, who would go on to write and direct Monster and director-writer Brian Dannelly and writer Michael Urban, the team behind Saved. And somewhere in the middle of it all, I realized I had fallen in love again. With making movies. With imagining what can be. With the infinite possibilities that can follow "FADE IN:." The next year, when Scott Frank and Callie Khouri, who co-chaired the Screenwriting Department, decided to move on, Frank asked me to take their place.

There's little doubt that being able to answer the question, "So, what are you doing?" with "Frank Pierson asked me to chair the Screenwriting Program at AFI" carries some party conversation panache. But there are plenty of people who think that having an important-sounding job is the same as swimming in the shark pool, who float by you on their way to the bottom, eyes fixed, arms flopping "Follow me!" like dead Captain Ahab impaled by his own harpoon on the white whale. One day, while passionately making some oh-so-important point to a production team, I realized I was becoming that guy. The guy who talked the talk, but wasn't walking the walk. Or should I say, swimming the swim. Every word I said to a student suddenly seemed to me to be the last gasp of a drowning man, floating like bubbles toward the light....

What saved me was something Frank said to the new students at the opening ceremonies at AFI. In speaking of his own career, he remarked that he had been a working writer every day of his life for 40 years. He wasn't talking about jobs, which is something somebody else gives to you—or takes away. He was talking about being somebody who does the work of a writer. And that is writing. Which is what I wasn't doing. It wasn't enough to be in love with the endless possibilities of the movies. You had to do the hard work of trying to make a movie happen.

I stopped worrying about my career and just started writing.

If this were a Hollywood fairy tale, we would CUT TO: me in my seat at the Oscars® just as Halle Berry calls out my name for Best Original Screenplay, hoping to get a little Adrien Brody action from me. That hasn't happened—but I was nominated (for the second time) for the Humanitas Prize for an episode of *The Famous Jett Jackson*, which for some still obscure reason the executive producer, Bruce Kalish, himself an excellent writer, thought he couldn't write but I could. Okay, no Academy Award®, but how about this for a boffo finish? I sell a script for a million bucks. Well, the fact is that hasn't happened, either—but, recently, I did sell a script that I've been working on for six years to HBO; I have another making the rounds with two movie stars and a bankable director attached; and I just finished another spec that is going out with a highly successful producer in its genre attached. Maybe by the time you read this, one of those will have sold. Okay, fine. My own TV show: how big a fantasy is that? Sorry to disappoint you. Best I can report is that I was a producer of the Emmy®-winning Nightline/PBS documentary magazine series *Life 360*, hosted by the lovely and amazingly brilliant Michel Martin.

Sadly, the show was canceled after two seasons, but I'm as proud to have been a part of it as anything I've ever done.

Don't be disappointed. I know you want a big finish, so here it is:

I'm swimming again.

Maybe that's anticlimactic for you, but it works for me. Because I've discovered the ancient Romans were right: *docendo discimus.* We learn by teaching.

And I've learned that the way to accept the challenge of helping my students make their dreams come true is to not give up on mine. That you have to love the whole thing: the struggles with the successes; the rejections with the accolades. Because in the end, there is simply your work.

And there is no guarantee of where that will take you. There is no way around the infinite blankness of the empty page, save to fill it with something you believe to be true.

That's how you keep from drowning. You write. That is the act of faith that keeps you afloat, as you will see in the essays that follow....

# Felicia D. Henderson

## The Hottest Sitcom Writer in Hollywood

*"As I turn in my brilliant pilot script, my head is so big, I can barely fit into my small car (can't wait to get that S-Class)."*

One of eight children, Felicia D. Henderson, whose credits include *Family Matters*, *The Fresh Prince of Bel-Air* and *Soul Food*, grew up in Pasadena, CA, where she was raised by very Southern parents. Her entertaining family members provide the blueprint for most of the television and movie characters she creates.

I HAD ARRIVED! I was only 32 years old and for four-and-a-half months, in 1997, I was the hottest sitcom writer in all of Hollywood!

My genius agent had convinced a hot Producer/Director that I was the only writer in all of Hollywood who could possibly create the perfect sitcom world for a hot R&B Girl Group that the Producer/ Director had signed to a development deal. The R&B trio had practically made the comedy development executives swoon at one of the big three networks. And in case that wasn't enough, this hot girl group had videos in heavy rotation on MTV, BET and VH-1. The Record Company, also one of the big ones, is already promising theme music, a soundtrack, and hot musical guests for my hot sitcom.

A minor setback… upon hearing the hot Producer/Director's choice for a writer—me—the Network requests a face-to-face because they aren't sure I'm so hot. The Producer/Director accompanies me to the meeting and informs the Network that I'm the only writer he wants to work with. And with that, I'm still smokin'. The Network "approves" me to write the pilot!

While I'm writing, the word gets around town that I have a hot pilot with a hot Network with a hot Girl Group attached and suddenly I'm very popular. The Record Company sends limos to make sure that I get to the big parties. The hot Girl Group doesn't want to shoot their next video on a day that I'm not available to be there to hang out. From behind my Armani sunglasses with UV-400 protection, I explain to the Executive Producer of the sitcom I'm working on that he needs to lighten my load so I can write my hot pilot. He agrees (probably hoping I'll hire him one day).

It's difficult to focus on writing because I spend a lot of time daydreaming about my new Mercedes, the house I'm going to buy my mom, and the scholarship fund I'm going to set up for future female sitcom writers who want to be just like me. I'm dodging agents who're trying to steal me away from my genius agent. I'm dating a hot Record Producer, a friend of the big record company's A&R exec. (Due to our combined hotness, we're obviously the perfect couple.)

As I turn in my brilliant pilot script, my head is so big, I can barely fit into my small car (can't wait to get that S-Class). It's in the Network's hands now. But this is just a formality. The Studio loved my script, the Record Company loved my script, the Girl Group loved my script, the hot Producer/Director loved my script, and my genius agent loved my script.

I get the word that the Network is ready to give notes on my first draft. As I sit in the meeting waiting for the Network and Studio Execs to finish talking about shoes, I practice being gracious in my mind, until I hear the Network Exec speak. They don't know any African-Americans who act like my characters. They thought the script would be "funnier," full of more "high jinks." I start to hyperventilate, I become combative, defensive. The hot Producer/Director jumps in to save me from myself, suggesting that "we" go back and look at a rewrite. The Studio Exec concurs. "We'll" rewrite...

I write a completely new script and everyone's elated. I'm back on top! Now, I just have to wait for the official pickup in February. I keep partying, dating the hot Record Producer, listening to my genius agent's accolades, and making time for that sitcom that continues to pay me a sizable salary as the show's completely arrogant co-executive producer.

Finally, February arrives. Hallelujah! I start to hear about other pilots being picked up. But that's okay. I turned mine in a little later than most because I had to do that extensive, yet inspired, second draft. The word finally comes! First from my agent, then from my Studio... The Network is passing on my pilot. They couldn't find a place for it on their schedule. There was no companion-piece series with which to put it. My genius agent tells me how stupid Network Execs are.

I cry for 24 straight hours before losing all sense of decorum. I beg the Studio to send my script out to burgeoning weblets. They're desperate for quality work like mine. The smaller networks also pass on my pilot.

I call the hot Producer/Director. It takes a week for him to call me back. I quickly pitch my new pilot idea to him. It's perfect for HBO, where he has a great relationship. He politely tells me he doesn't have time for another TV project right now. He's about to direct a big-budget movie for my Studio. At that time, I realize I haven't heard from the A&R exec in a couple of weeks. I call him four times before he calls me back. I ask him about the huge Puff Daddy party that's coming up. He says he'll try to "hustle around" for an invitation for me. He doesn't call back. My soul mate, the hot Record Producer, drops me. It's a bad time for him to be in a serious relationship.

Just as the condolence phone calls stop, I get one last call from the supportive Studio Exec who wants to help me be okay with this. The Exec tells me the Network found me difficult to work with, combative, unwilling to take notes, which made them uncomfortable giving me notes, which means they never really told me exactly what they wanted from my pilot... But for four-and-a-half months, in 1997, I was the hottest sitcom writer in all of Hollywood!

**EPILOGUE**: In 1999, I got another chance to create a television series. This time I wasn't nearly as "hot" in my own mind. I worked a lot harder—no parties, no dates for three months, and I wrote 12 hours a day. That one-hour drama, *Soul Food*, based on the 1997 hit film of the same name, is now in its third highly—rated and critically—acclaimed season on the Showtime Network. I still have the same genius agent and a development deal with the same wonderful Studio.

# Lionel Chetwynd

## Me And The Monster

---

*"'Fuck you, Otto,' I smiled warmly."*

Lionel Chetwynd, writer of *Ike, The Siege at Ruby Ridge* and *The Apprenticeship of Duddy Kravitz*, has over 40 long-form credits that have garnered many awards, including an Oscar® nomination and a WGA award (five nominations). He serves on The President's Committee on the Arts and Humanities.

The carpet was deep-piled white cashmere shag, so popular amongst the ridiculously wealthy of the mid-'70s. The walls were white, elegant matte finish punctuated by huge, brilliantly colored DeBuffets and Modiglianis. Even the New York skyline that lay beyond the windows of this 22-floor Columbia Pictures Headquarters glistened white. In the middle of the room was a raised dais, perhaps ten feet square and two feet high. It, too, was white, as was the marble desk upon it. And behind the desk, ensconced in a huge white suede chair, was the Emperor: Otto Preminger.

I sat in the white leather guest chair, peering up at Otto on his Mussolini platform, desperate not to reveal my inner terror by a shaking hand or dry mouth. Not that it mattered; Otto, like all feral

---

215

beasts, could smell fear. This was not my first freelance gig, but it was the first since leaving a regular job. I was young, we had two children hardly more than infants, and I needed to keep this assignment that paid weekly. I had been warned by older, wiser heads that Otto destroyed people for fun, particularly writers. But I had the assurance of youth and the certainty that comes with a young man's passions. "Ah, well," Carl Foreman had shrugged, "perhaps you will be the one to tame the tiger. Just remember: Otto never hears the sound of his own voice..."

I had failed—woefully—to tame even the tiger's office staff, let alone him. He had lived up to the most awful of the predictions. He was a hard and unforgiving man who enjoyed terrorizing all who came near him—particularly writers, especially writers. William Goldman, whom I had met in London, had befriended me when he learned I was in Otto's indentured servitude, and would take me to lunch three or more times a week. He explained, "Otto hates writers most because he can't write himself. You'll find that in a lot of producers and directors."

"What do I do?"

The Master shrugged, smiled softly. "Always protect that part of you that writes."

And, sitting in the dazzlingly bright room, that would be my task—to survive the next half hour with the part of me that writes intact.

I had come into Otto's service because he wanted the rights to a book I had previously acquired, the story of Henry Norman Bethune, a Canadian doctor who had gone from the Spanish Civil War to China, accompanied Mao on the Long Route March, and became the only person mentioned by name in Mao Tse-Tung's famous Little Red Book. (My view of political virtue has changed since the '70s....) Trudeau's Canada had recently normalized relations with the People's Republic and Otto wanted to be the first to shoot in what, at that time, was a deeply mysterious place. I had transferred the rights with the commitment that I would be the screenwriter. On that basis, Gloria and I and our kids moved back from London to America, living as modestly as possible in the suburbs while building this new career.

It had been a nightmare. From Day One. Otto would terrorize, tease, taunt, demean, embarrass and humiliate all who came near— and a writer in a notes meeting is unbearably near.

That morning was especially painful. As a weekly writer, I delivered pages daily, and we had become mired in a scene where Bethune was living in a *ménage à trois*, and Otto hated every stab I made at revealing the tensions. It had become clear that this was his particular fantasy, and until the tensions were replaced by a profusion of naked, damp bodies intertwined, he'd never be happy.

The night before, he had thrown my pages in my face and ordered that I rewrite overnight and present him with a "correct" scene or he would fire me and have me arrested for grand larceny for having presented myself as a writer. Such was the impaler's thrall, I'd actually called the Guild to see if such a thing was possible. "Of course not," they told me. But they lived in the normal world and I worked for Otto.

I had stayed up all night crafting the words on the empty page—again and again, refining, polishing, rethinking. In that precomputer night, I must have run through a ream of paper. As dawn broke, I stared at the telephone, waiting until the hour was decent enough to call someone, read them the scene, ask their help.

By 6 a.m., the pain was too great. I dialed my Agent's home number, began reading as soon as he answered. "Sounds great to me," said Leo. "But I'm only an agent. What do I know? Besides, the man's insane."

Leo was right. He was an agent, not a screenwriter. 6:32 a.m. Almost a full sun in the sky. Somewhere a dog barked, an early-morning commuter's car coughed to life.

I presumed on a delicate friendship, dialed a number, and woke Bill Goldman. He understood. He empathized. He listened calmly as I read the four-and-a-half pages. A brief silence. And then, "Lionel, that's as good as I might do myself. Present the pages with confidence. With pride. And protect that part of you that writes."

Five minutes later, I handed them to Otto who had grunted, "Are they any good?" I failed to answer quickly enough with Bill Goldman's advice, and Otto had snorted with derision, cutting me off with, "You see, you are a failure and a fraud. A true writer would have pride and confidence in his work. You are... you are..."

He had shrugged as if unable to find a phylum low enough to accommodate me, then put the pages in front of him, hunched over them, began reading. I watched with mixed dread and hope. The rent was due next week. We were broke. Please love them. Please. I *need* this job. Gloria's out of work, we can't feed the kids if you don't like—

But he smiled at what he read. He glanced up, looked at me while a trace of a grin was still visible—barely, but definitely there. My heart soared. On to page two. A similar reaction. A broader smile, a better grin. So too, page three. I was going to survive!

Until page four. His face contorted in Hitlerian fury, spittle formed at the corners of his mouth, veins throbbed on his signature bald head, his eyes popped out. He screwed the pages into a ball, threw them at me. I ducked, prayed he'd regain control.

He did. He smiled the cold smile of a Prussian Aristocrat.

"Chetta-veend," he whispered in his deceptively soft High German accent. "Life is a curious thing, you know? For example, all my life I have felt we are too free with gun laws in this country. And you see, that is because in America, anybody might own an instrument of death."

I wasn't sure where this was going, but I didn't like it. "Instrument of death," huh? If anyone I knew in the world had one of those, it was the bald-headed *Junker* across—actually perched above—me.

He continued. "You see, Chetta-veend, in such a regime, I might have here..." He paused, and indicated the small (white) cabinet of drawers beside him. "...a weapon. A firearm."

No. He couldn't. Not even this ogre. But he opened the top drawer. I thought I heard something heavy go "clump" as it slid forward.

"And, provoked as I am by your failure and, in a righteous rage at your uselessness to humanity, I would reach into this drawer for that firearm..."

God save me, he put his hand in the drawer. This time, I definitely heard a heavy thud. My palms sweated, I was gripped by an urge to flee but seemed unable to move. It was all happening so fast, yet in slow-motion.

"And I would remove that weapon—no doubt a finely made

German Luger pistol that never misfires..."

The sonuvabitch was about to murder me. Suddenly, in rapid fire:

"And-I-would-remove-the-pistol—"

I saw him take something dark and heavy from that drawer. He had finally lost control, and I was to become a headline. I wouldn't even get decent billing given the murderer was Otto. As he raised the object, I did what the Army had taught me to do: I hit the floor, crossing my arms over my chest, rolling side-over-side until I was behind the only available cover—the chair I had been sitting in a split second ago.

A beat of silence. And then a strange buzzing sound. I peered around the edge of the chair.

The heavy object was a Remington Cordless Razor. Otto was shaving his head.

"I have decided you might as well live long enough to try one last time. Get back to your office."

I stood up, turned to do his bidding.

And then I remembered: protect that part of me that writes.

"Fuck you, Otto," I smiled warmly. "I quit."

The morning air of Fifth Avenue never smelled sweeter.

# Ann Marcus

## *Mary Hartman, Mary Hartman:* It Was the Best of Times, The Worst of Times

*"I hadn't run screaming from the room."*

Ann Marcus has written thousands of credited on-air scripts over a career that spans 40 years and counting. She has co-created several series, including *Julie Farr, MD*; *Mary Hartman, Mary Hartman*; *All That Glitters* and *Fernwood 2Nite*. She won an Emmy® for *Mary Hartman* and the WGA Award for *Search for Tomorrow*.

I think I was the writer of last resort on Norman Lear's new project in 1975, and I got to see him through the back door. Well, maybe it was the side door. At any rate he had just about given up trying to find a writer to implement his idea for a very different kind of soap opera, even though his stubborn chief of staff, Al Burton, kept looking. Al ran into my agent in the men's room of the Beverly Wilshire Hotel and that's how I got to meet Norman. Not in the men's room, but in his office where he explained his concept: a soap on two levels. One level would satirize the medium, the other would hook the audience with characters and stories on a realistic level.

Obviously since it was a Norman Lear project, the stories would be controversial—all Norman's shows were. But with *Mary*

*Hartman*, Norman wanted to be outrageous!

The concept sounded logical enough; the soap would be built around an auto worker's family—Tom, his wife Mary, their adolescent child, plus Mary's parents, sister and neighbors—a typical, ordinary, blue-collar family living in a small Ohio town. But there was a stipulation. It was what Norman insisted on happening the first week of the soap. And it was so bizarre that it had driven half the comedy writers in Hollywood screaming from his office. They heard the pitch and told him: a) it wasn't funny; b) it wouldn't work; c) he'd never get it on the air; d) if by some chance he did get it on the air nobody would watch it; and e) "Let me outta here!"

So what was this vision of Norman's that had freaked out all those writers? He wanted to open with the mass murder of a neighborhood family, including their goats and chickens.

It was Norman's litmus test. If, on hearing this outrageous opening, a writer used any of the a) through e) comments, the meeting was over. I wanted the job so bad, I sat glued to the chair and when it was over I did not bolt. I did not gasp. I even managed to laugh.

"Wonderful," I said. "What a great way to start," I added shamelessly, intuitively realizing that Norman, like every other writer I've ever known including myself, loved to be flattered.

I hadn't run screaming from the room. I passed the test. I was given the material that had already been created by novelist and comedy writer Gail Parent, who had come up with the original concept of dramatizing the everyday life of a dysfunctional auto worker's family. But after creating the members of Mary's family— her bored auto worker husband, Tom; her libidinous sister, Cathy;

and clueless parents—Gail left on a long book tour and had nothing more to do with the show.

In the coming weeks as I struggled to create story lines, flesh out the family, and invent the neighborhood characters, I realized those other freaked-out writers who had failed the test were right. There isn't anything funny about the massacre of a family of five— even or especially if their goats and chickens are included.

I wasn't having much fun and Norman wasn't much help. He was busy with his other shows, and he had so many negative reactions about the concept from other writers that I don't think he felt I could bring it off. Neither did I. I knew I needed help. So I recruited Daniel Gregory Browne and Jerry Adelman, both of whom had worked with me before and whose weird, eclectic sense of the absurd fit in perfectly with the style of the show. The three of us solved the problem of how to make the mass murder palatable and even funny by not showing it and having Mary so involved with the waxy yellow buildup on her kitchen floor that she hardly notices the sound of the wailing sirens as they race by offstage.

After Daniel, Jerry and I finished writing the Bible (the long-term stories), we wrote ten half-hour comedy scripts (the series was on five times a week). The pilot consisted of the first two half-hours, which included the massacre, Grandpa Larkin's flashing, and Tom's problem with impotence. The networks wouldn't touch it, but after some very innovative marketing, Norman found enough independent stations to get it on the air.

Even before it premiered, a great deal of publicity had been generated in which we writers weren't even mentioned. It was Norman Lear's show all the way down the line. According to the media, he had created the whole thing. Daniel, Jerry and I were some "veteran soap writers" who had filled in the numbers.

That made me mad. So I challenged Norman about it, and the wonderful thing about Norman is that if you confront him with the truth, he agrees with you. He's not defensive; he doesn't try to blame someone else; he simply does the right thing—or in this case, almost the right thing. A day or two after our meeting, this full-page ad appeared in the trades:

FIRST CAME THE WORD

The "veteran soap writers" widely credited with having something to do with *Mary Hartman, Mary Hartman* are in fact the very gifted, insightful and vastly experienced…

ANN MARCUS
DANIEL GREGORY BROWNE
JERRY ADELMAN

And the ad went on to mention the "brilliant directorial talents of Joan Darling and Jim Drake" and the actors.

So why did I say he "almost" did the right thing? Because even though he said we were talented, he failed to mention that we were co-creators of the show, having invented most of the characters and written the pilot and story lines. Am I quibbling? I don't think so; credits are a writer's best friend. So much so that I blew a chance to give enough credit to the late Daniel Gregory Browne who was so important to the creation of the show. We shared the "created by" credit, but I also had another credit: Head Writer. Dan wanted another credit, too: From The Neck Down. But I was too uptight to go for it, although I wish I had.

*Mary Hartman* premiered on January 6, 1976. My husband Ellis and I hosted a small party at the house to watch it. Jerry and Dan were there as we lowered the lights and turned on the set. The corny theme music started and Dody Goodman's voice could be heard from our collective childhoods calling out "Mary Hartman, Mary Hartman." We were off on the most exhilarating and exhausting experience of our lives.

We knew it was good, but we weren't prepared for the overwhelming reaction to it. *MH2* wasn't just a hit, it was a megahit. In no time, it became addictive, a "pop culture craze" as *Newsweek* put it, "a sort of video Rorschach test for the mass audience." Everyone was talking about it or writing about it. Critics were comparing it to the best of Chekhov, Cervantes, James Joyce, John Updike and Ingmar Bergman. Louise Lasser as Mary Hartman stared out from the covers of every popular, glossy, high and lowbrow periodical in the country. And inside, there were long analytical pieces on the meaning of it all.

The more successful the show became, the more interested Norman became in it and the more time he spent with us. In the very beginning, Dan and Jerry and I had been left pretty much on our own as we wrote the first weeks of scripts. But once the show was in production and especially after it enjoyed such a spectacular reception, Norman neglected his other shows to spend hours and hours and hours with us. This was both wonderful and terrible.

We had daily story conferences which were tape recorded and ran into 80 or more pages of transcripts, keeping an army of typists at work through the night. But there were only three of us writing five scripts each week, and what with participating in marathon story meetings, reading the manuscripts, writing the outlines and then the scripts, we were always in a state of hysterical exhaustion.

On the other hand, Norman, who wasn't writing scripts or

outlines, remained fresh as a daisy and very funny and inventive. He was especially fond of thinking up quirky ways to eliminate characters he grew tired of. When he decided Coach Leroy Fedder should go, he came up with drowning him in a huge bowl of Mary's chicken soup.

During the last episode of the season—the 126th episode— Mary/Louise gave a bravura performance and went bonkers on *The David Susskind Show*. She ended up in the Fernwood hospital for the mentally challenged.

Daniel, Jerry and I almost joined her there, but instead we were awarded Emmys® for "outstanding individual achievement."

# Jane Anderson

## My Dark And Sordid Past

*"It taught me humility, which believe it or not, is a writer's most important tool."*

Jane Anderson is a playwright, television writer, actress, director and screenwriter. Her TV credits include *The Positively True Adventures of the Alleged Texas Cheerleader-Murdering Mom, The Baby Dance, If These Walls Could Talk 2, When Billie Beat Bobby* and *Normal*. Her film credits include *How to Make an American Quilt* and *The Prize Winner of Defiance, Ohio*.

There are a few credits from my past that I've tried to blot from my record. Those of us who write the so-called "serious" stuff are loath to admit that we've ever written anything but feature films or movies for your more prestigious cable networks. And of course, theater—we serious writers always, but always "developed our craft" in the theater.

That is my myth. But the truth is, I started my career as a professional writer on a sitcom called *The Facts of Life*. For those of you who aren't familiar with this show (and I wasn't either when I first took the job), *The Facts of Life* was a long-running sitcom about four fun girls in a boarding school under the care of Charlotte Rae, who played the whacky yet warm headmistress. I had just moved to L.A. from New York and was still trying to make my mark as an actress/ comic (as opposed to comic actress). I had been performing a comedy act which I'd written myself and while I was waiting to be dubbed the next Lily Tomlin, I wrote a spec script so I could find meaningful employment. I landed the *Facts* job mostly because the producers were desperate for female writers in a market where male comedy writers still outnumbered the gals 10 to 1.

I truly hated the job. I'm not a very good gang writer and I felt morally compromised during every miserable hour I sat at the table punching up lines (I had just come from New York, after all, and was still a cultural snob). The showrunner was a Scientologist who smoked in the room and relieved his boredom by spearing pencils into the acoustic ceiling. Most of the staff were guys who were at an utter loss as to how to write for the four teenage stars and so kept themselves amused by telling jokes about tits, butts, farts, penises, vaginas, homosexuals and fat people. One day, the showrunner told a joke about African-Americans that was so offensive it made my jaw drop. When I tried to bust him on it, he said, "Hey, Jane, it's OK, I got a Humanitas Award."

I quit the show after a season and a half and went off to write a play. It was my first full-length play and one of my best, I think. The fact is, my time on that sitcom had taught me a craft. I learned how to take an idea, go off in a corner, and come back with ten cogent pages of script. I learned to take notes on those pages and come back with ten more. And more importantly, I learned how to throw it all out, without resentment, fear or regret, and start all over again. That sitcom was my boot camp for learning the art of revision. It gave me the stamina to take a script from a callow first draft to something worthy of production. It taught me humility, which believe it or not, is a writer's most important tool. Humility leaves you open to new ideas. It keeps you hungry, keeps you fresh. It keeps the muse engaged.

There was another regular on *The Facts of Life*, the one lone male presence in the show. The character's name was George, a good-looking but ineffectual fellow who seemed to have no reason for being in any of the scenes except maybe for visual relief. I remember being on the set and watching this actor dutifully follow his blocking, in vain search of a motivation. I felt bad for him because none of us writers had a clue of what to do with his character and he was clearly doomed to be in a plot limbo for the rest of the series. The young actor was George Clooney and he's done just fine for himself. Not only is he a star, he's also an astoundingly good director. I'm sure he's been just as embarrassed by that credit as I have been by mine. But God knows what valuable stuff he must have learned on that set. Clearly, he never played a piece of window dressing again.

So yes, there are no bad credits, only bad, snotty attitudes. Entertainment is entertainment and, yes, I accept the time I worked on *The Facts of Life* as something fine and valuable. I own it, I celebrate it, I embrace it as part of my past. Now... can we move on?

●●●●●●●●●●●●●●●●●●●●●●●●●●●●

# SECRETS OF THE HOLLYWOOD PROS #6:

## Rejecting Rejection

●●●●●●●●●●●●●●●●●●●●●●●●●●●●

**There's No Cure: The struggles of the writer's life are chronic but not fatal.**

Dennis Palumbo, MA, MFCC, is a writer-turned-therapist, whose insights into the psychology of being a writer can be found each month in *Written By*, the journal of the Writers Guild of America, West, from which this article is excerpted. We're pleased to have the doctor in this volume:

🔹
🔹

I have a book called *Writing From the Inside Out*. Needless to say, I'm very excited about it. Getting a book published isn't something that happens every day. Plus, I'm grateful for the opportunity to expand on the issues I've talked about in *Written By* and to explore in greater depth the various problems faced by all writers everywhere. As an added bonus, Larry Gelbart was gracious enough to write the foreword to the book.

So much for the good stuff.

---

There's another side to the book's publication I have to talk about. After all, I've been a professional writer for more than 20 years and have been in private practice as a psychotherapist treating creative people for a dozen more. I've counseled writers through the turmoil of publication, the anxiety of movie premieres, the brutality of staffing season. I've helped them struggle with writer's block, procrastination, and fear. I've consoled them in the face of an agent's neglect, a producer's rejection, an editor's disrespect, and an industry's indifference.

I mean, let's face it: I know the drill.

So, how has it been for me, now just another writer with a product about to hit the marketplace? If anyone should be able to handle the expected pragmatic and emotional challenges, it's me. Right?

Guess again. In the months leading up to my book's release date, I have obsessed about the book's title; fantasized one minute about getting on the best-seller's list and then in the next was absolutely convinced that no one would buy it at all; yearned for my agent to be more understanding, supportive, and devoted to my personal and professional well-being to the exclusion of all else in his life; already mentally answered potential bad reviews with pithy, scathing rejoinders; seen my editor's decision to leave my publisher for another job in the middle of working on my book as a "sign" that the universe is plotting against me; ditto the above, when I learned that my publisher had listed my book's title incorrectly in its catalog; felt unloved, abandoned, and unappreciated when a friend even looked like he was anything less than totally thrilled or profoundly moved at the thought of my book coming out.

Believe me, I could go on, but space doesn't permit. The point is that despite the knowledge and insight gained from long-time careers as both a writer and therapist, I find myself wrestling with the same dilemmas I always have.

## Publish & Perish

**Like it or not, when you're a writer, there's no escaping the writer's life.**

I'm reminded of that scene from *Godfather III*, when crime boss Al Pacino, failing to extricate himself from his professional obligations, wails, "Just when I thought I was out, they pull me back in!" Throughout the film his efforts to enter legitimate business were an attempt to leave behind the events and experiences of his former life.

My own career transition from screenwriter to psychotherapist, I must have believed at some level, was supposed to afford me the same consolation. I was finally "out" of the business, freed from the day-to-day struggles of a Hollywood writer. No longer having to battle studio execs about material or my own inner demons about my ability.

But, as I've learned with the sale of my book, when it comes to the feelings, obsessions, and just plain worries that accompany any writer's efforts, there's no getting out. Regardless of career experience, advancing age, and sizable amounts of therapy, there's no "cure" for the writer's life. As soon as writers commit to the writing of a thing, they embark on a journey through both an external world of crises and triumphs and an internal world of feelings and belief systems.

And this is true for all writers, no matter their level of success, no matter how vast their audience, how large and loyal their readership. I say as much at the end of my book. I posit two simple facts: first, that all successful writers once were struggling ones, and, second, that the successful ones still struggle. This is not merely philosophical ruminating on my part. As my recent experience attests, this is the straight dope. One of those hard truths of life. Bedrock.

On the other hand, I've negotiated the psychological rigors of publication about as well as can be expected. As a writer and a therapist, I've learned, and changed, a lot during the years, and it's definitely made a difference.

The biggest change? Probably this: In many ways I'm as neurotic and insecure as I ever was. I just don't hassle myself about it anymore. And although that might not be a cure, it's the next best thing.

Formerly a Hollywood screenwriter (*My Favorite Year, Welcome Back, Kotter*), Dennis Palumbo is now a licensed psychotherapist specializing in creative issues. *Writing From the Inside Out: Transforming Your Psychological Blocks to Release the Writer Within*, a book based on his *Written By* columns, is available from John Wiley & Sons.

# THE ECSTASY

# Chapter 7

## INTRODUCTION

## They Like Me, They Really Like Me:

## Coming Out the Other End

My favorite writer acceptance speech came one night at the Writers Guild Awards when Alfred Uhry, who won the award for Best Original Screenplay for *Driving Miss Daisy*, thanked his agent for sticking with him through the nearly 20-year process of becoming an overnight success.

In that speech, Urhy invoked one of the fundamental rules of being a screenwriter: it's a struggle. In the long run—and, for most, it is a long run even to be in it for the short run—that struggle will call your sanity into question, exhaust your will and all of your close relationships, leaving you tilting at windmills with no Sancho Panza and scant hope of a Dulcinea.

So why do it? The glib answer is that they might be giants. But, if you have gotten this far in this book, you know that screenwriting is a craft, a business and a commitment—not a lottery open to anyone with screenwriting software and a penchant for magical thinking. The real answer, the one that sustains committed writers on their quest, is the belief expressed by Phil Alden Robinson in his screenplay for *Field of Dreams*: "If you build it, they will come..."

The key, as you will learn from our next writers, is to build something that matters to you. And to build it well....

# Jessica Bendinger

## The Agony and the Ecstasy

---

*"…when I stopped staring at my diploma from Hollywood U. and explored a life beyond screenplays, my career did not improve—it took off."*

Jessica Bendinger's credits include *Bring It On*, *The Truth About Charlie*, *First Daughter* and *Sex and the City*. Her uncredited work as a script doctor continues to amaze her parents, given her absolute lack of medical training.

If you are fortunate enough to have a career in Hollywood, you'll soon discover that means equal parts agony and ecstasy. The waiting can be agonizing: for an idea, a response, a decision, a breakthrough. And the highs can be ecstatic: a green light, a great review, a big opening weekend. Success in Hollywood doesn't eliminate or guarantee life on one end of the spectrum. It demands that you learn to harmonize with both.

Hollywood is like Power University. Those who enroll can learn how to use power, misuse it, envy it, wield it, withhold it, share it and enjoy it. You can earn units towards graduation in lots of ways, but power is the coveted degree. And writers are particularly vulnerable to its charms.

Because if you're a writer, you already think you're not good enough. So a professor with a Doctorate in Power telling you, "You're brilliant!" is like gin to a jones. You didn't know exactly how bad your DTs were until somebody started spoon-feeding you the good stuff: approval. And approval is the cheapest street drug Tinsel Town can offer you. It's free, it's in voluminous supply and it creates new junkies every day.

Undergrads and Ph. D.s in Writing all have minors in Not Good Enough. You might even believe it because writers are editors. And the constant revising can drive you down Low Self-Esteem Lane faster than a Gulfstream will get you from Van Nuys to Burbank. And when you live in a state of constant revision, you can start believing that you are never good enough. That who you are and what you write will never be a perfect draft. And you'd be right.

The revisions never end. There's always another note, another draft, another tweak or another writer to remind you just how Not Good Enough you really are. And making things work on paper doesn't mean you know how to make them work in your life. Far from it! So when your dreams come true, just look out. You can quickly discover that your reality hasn't come true at all. When your career gets healthy, you can discover that your life is severely dehydrated.

And fixing a malnourished script is a lot easier than finding an IV for an anemic life. After isolating with a computer and being rewarded for that isolation, figuring out what enjoyment means can be disorienting. After all, the monikers we're spoon-fed about artists aren't that sweet: Starving Artist! Tortured Artist! Neurotic Writer! Blocked Writer! The culture is mired in completely clichéd ideas about what constitutes a creative life and an artistic spirit. And your spirit can get sick and tired of it.

How do you pull off self-to-self resuscitation? How do you swing from talking only to yourself, your computer and your dog to being in the world and in your life? It's different for everyone, and I'm still figuring it out. I wish there were a one-size-fits-all solution, but that's the good news: writing and editing sets writers up for successful experimentation. Trying things differently and seeking new experiences are imperative to the creative process. And that exploration will get you from a blank page to a written stack faster than banging your head against the screen.

So when you finally get your cap and gown and move your tassel and collect that diploma and frame it and hang it on your wall, remember this: nobody will care about your life if you don't. And it just might help your work. Because when I stopped staring at my diploma from Hollywood U. and explored a life beyond screenplays, my career did not improve—it took off.

# Donna Powers & Wayne Powers

## No Room For Cynicism

---

*"We both realize that this is a moment to savor and that there is nothing more Hollywood than being on Hollywood Boulevard and* blowing shit up.*"*

Donna and Wayne Powers live in Los Angeles with their son, Austin. Their credits include *Deep Blue Sea* (shared with Duncan Kennedy), *The Italian Job* and *Skeletons in the Closet* (which Wayne also directed). They also created, wrote and executive produced *Out of Order*, a six-hour Showtime limited series, of which Wayne directed three hours.

A girl of ten, from Birmingham, Alabama, stood on Hollywood Boulevard in front of Grauman's Chinese Theater, looking at all the stars engraved with famous names on the sidewalk, the handprints of cinema legends in the cement. Two years later, a boy of 12 from rural New Hampshire stood there, too, dreaming of living in Los Angeles and making movies.

Untold years later, that boy and girl have become us and we are both standing in the very same spot. Only now, the five blocks that surround the famed movie theater are closed off to traffic, replaced with picture cars. And the tourists have been replaced with hundreds of extras, while real tourists stand behind ropes, taking Instamatic pictures, perhaps thinking that they had

---

242

stumbled upon a typical day in Hollywood. As the third take of a scene unfolds, a crane lifts higher, a series of explosions roars around an armored truck, and two helicopters shatter the air above the turbo-throb. This is the 45th shooting day of the remake of *The Italian Job*, a heist movie we wrote, starring Mark Wahlberg, Edward Norton, Charlize Theron, and Donald Sutherland.

We both realize that this is a moment to savor and that there is nothing more Hollywood than being on Hollywood Boulevard and *blowing shit up*.

The original movie took place in Rome, and when the studio decided to relocate it to America they suggested San Francisco; nonetheless, they were pleasantly surprised when we delivered a draft that took place in Los Angeles, the draft that got the movie "greenlit." We chose L.A. because it seemed like an ironic place to create a huge traffic jam and also because we knew we could write to location. So we rode the Metro Rail to figure out the escape route that Wahlberg's crew would take, and scoured the city for cool spots for the action. We also picked L.A. because it was going through a film-production drought. This led to one of the *best feelings* a screenwriter can have: watching hundreds of people busily working and bringing paychecks home because of something we had written.

Cut to a month later, and we are filming an intimate, intense dramatic scene with Eric Stoltz and William H. Macy for *Out of Order*, a highly personal series that we've created for Showtime. In tone and in every imaginable way, the two projects are completely different from each other. But there is one great similarity: once again, we are able to look around and see scores of people gainfully employed because of something that began with us putting pen to paper. It's the best.

Back to *The Italian Job* set. We are welcomed and respected. We have chairs in front of the monitors with our names on them; we are given headsets to hear the dialogue and earplugs to avoid hearing the explosions. The producer, Donald De Line, coaxes us to work, of course—polishing some dialogue here, making revisions there—but he makes us feel respected and included when he is on the phone to the head of Paramount and talks about the fact that the Powers are on set and tells him all the ways that we're helping out. The director of photography chats with us. The production designer proudly shows off his work. The director, F. Gary Gray, looking like a kid in a candy store, gives us high-fives as we have our picture taken with him in front of the shot-up armored truck. In between setups, we shoot the breeze with Mark Wahlberg while he shoots baskets outside his trailer.

Just like anyone in any profession, writers often talk cynically about their work. But for us, a girl from Alabama and a boy from New Hampshire, to be able to stand on Hollywood Boulevard and remember when we were just kids, before we found and married each other, before becoming writing partners; to remember when we could only dream about being right here and making movies, well, there is no room for cynicism on this day.

# Mary Agnes Donoghue

## From the Front

---

*"Perhaps the writer had a vision, too."*

A native New Yorker, Mary Agnes Donoghue divides her time between Los Angeles, London and the southwest of France. In between flights, she wrote and directed the film *Paradise*, wrote original screenplays for the films *Deceived* and *The Buddy System* and adapted the novels *Beaches* and *White Oleander* into films. Her stage play *Me and Mamie O'Rourke* ran at the Strand Theatre in London's West End.

I was hesitant about contributing an essay to this collection because, like most writers in Hollywood, apart from the act of writing itself and the fact that I am well paid, my experience has been repetitive rather than unique and has rarely made me happy. And like the majority of my comrades in arms, I recount my little tales of betrayal and disappointment too often and with the same kind of tired pride seen in highly experienced soldiers of fortune still searching for the right war.

Which is a very elaborate way of describing a whiner and I don't like being a whiner. So I'm going to tell a happy rather than a sad story, about the time I was asked to direct my own material because every director worth having had turned the project down and the studio decided to take a revolutionary approach and turn the execution of the material over to the person who had actually written it. I assume they did it on the off chance that the writer, more than anyone else, might actually know what the movie was about and would deliver dailies based on the script they had read in preproduction rather than on pages which had been feverishly rewritten by stars and directors the night before they were to be shot (with help, of course, from their loyal hairdressers, assistants and drivers).

It was an outrageous assumption, a dangerous one, one that could start a creative revolution. Could it be? Perhaps, just perhaps, the writer was not an indentured servant. Perhaps the writer had a vision, too.

I don't quite know why this happened, maybe because I begged shamelessly, but one day I got a call from Jeffrey Katzenberg during which he asked if I thought I could direct the movie. Without hesitation I said yes. I later asked my husband if I should tell them I'd never spent more than five minutes on a movie set. Without hesitation he said no. Several months later, I was in preproduction, but only after interviewing several prominent directors on their work methods. The people who understood best what I needed to know were Robert Wise and Richard Rush. One started as an editor, the other as a writer. Neither one of them ever mentioned art. Robert Wise told me where to leave my coat in the morning and how to run the set economically and effectively, and Richard Rush said there were three movies to be made—the one I wrote, the one I shot and the one I edited.

It was a daunting but fine experience and, even with all its flaws (due to my staggering inexperience), of all the films I've had made, *Paradise* comes the closest to being what I had intended it to be when I wrote it. Even stars are reluctant to ask a director to rewrite his own script, which meant I was never forced to rewrite good material simply because it was not understood; I only rewrote what didn't work. It was creative heaven.

Which thought brings me to a current war story I would like to tell as it has classic proportions. A movie I wrote is now being shot in Dublin. It is a script I'm proud of, the lead is being played by the perfect person, and I would be very happy had I not heard that the director, who joined the project after the perfect person had been cast, was restructuring the script himself only days before starting to shoot. A short time after receiving that disturbing news, I was sent a very expensive Il Bisonte script binder as a gift from the producer. Heartbroken and uncertain as to which script belonged in my lovely new binder, mine or the reconstructed one, I suddenly glanced down and noticed that my name, which was beautifully embossed into the soft, creamy leather, had been misspelled.

Ah, well. It's time to move on to the next war. I can always have the binder made into a purse.

# John August

## Are You Somebody?

*"Almost apologetically, I said I was a screenwriter."*

John August's screenwriting credits include *Go*, *Big Fish*, *Titan A.E.*, *Corpse Bride*, *Charlie's Angels*, *Charlie's Angels: Full Throttle* and *Charlie and the Chocolate Factory*. He maintains a screenwriting-oriented website at johnaugust.com.

There are no famous screenwriters.

There are rich screenwriters with houses in Malibu. There are acclaimed screenwriters with awards on their mantels. But none of them are actually famous. Your aunt in Pittsburgh can't name a single screenwriter—except for you, her little champ, working so hard to make it in Hollywood.

She's proud of you, but worries. Who wouldn't?

True, there are the hyphenates: writer-directors can be famous, not to mention actor-writer-directors, whose many hats only add to their publicity value. But no one gets famous just for writing 120 pages of 12-point Courier. You should know this going in, because if you have any interest in becoming "a household name," your best bet is to pick a pseudonym like Crisco or Clorox.

Here's an example of someone who is actually famous: Drew

Barrymore. A few years ago, paparazzi took pictures of us having lunch. In the caption, I was the "unidentified companion."

I wasn't offended, honest. By this point, I had fully accepted that I would never be recognized. The more time you spend with actual famous people, the more you realize that it pretty much sucks to have random people taking your picture or asking for autographs while your dog is pooping at Runyon Canyon Park.

Well-paid anonymity is a luxury, frankly. I came to enjoy it.

And then one day, someone recognized me.

My boyfriend and I were at LAX, flying to Colorado for Christmas vacation, with both our dogs in carriers. Out of nowhere, a young guy on crutches came up to me and stuck out his hand: "I just wanted to say, I'm a big fan." I stammered and thanked him, then went back to my dogs.

At the time, I was busy promoting *Big Fish*, so I figured that Crutches Guy had been at one of the countless Q&A screenings. He'd seen the film, liked it, and remembered me as the guy sitting next to Danny DeVito. I was flattered, and enjoyed the little jolt of adrenaline, but quickly wrote it off as a one-time thing.

But it wasn't.

As I've done more publicity, and talking-head interviews on various DVDs, I've found that random people are recognizing me and saying hello with increasing frequency. It's once a month or so—nothing alarming—but it always comes when I least it expect it: shopping for strollers, in line at the movies, at breakfast with the woman carrying my baby.

The hand-shakers are invariably polite, so I can always

genuinely say, "It's nice to meet you." But what's fascinating is how everyone around us reacts. Remember: as a screenwriter, I'm not actually famous. Yet suddenly someone is treating me like I am. I love watching that double take as bystanders try to figure out who I could possibly be.

Once, a nearby woman actually asked me, "Are you somebody?"

Almost apologetically, I said I was a screenwriter. Her face showed a combination of confusion and disappointment that would have been devastating at another point in my life.

While I stand by my no-famous-screenwriters rule, I need to issue a clarification. It is apparently possible to be recognizable among the subset of "aspiring screenwriters living in Los Angeles." That's far short of famous, but quite a bit better, in my opinion. Screenwriters are commendable folk. (Except for one guy who asked me to sign his hat, then dissed me in his blog.)

If there's a downside to being recognized, it's that occasionally I get half-recognized. At a restaurant, people will see me and know that they know me from somewhere. Throughout the rest of their meal, they will steal glances, wracking their brains to figure out who I could be. A musician? A contestant on *The Apprentice?* The Neo-Nazi from last night's *West Wing?* By the time salads arrive, I can feel their growing frustration.

So I take off my glasses.

With 18 inches of vision, the rest of the world blurs out, leaving me alone in my happy anonymity. Unless that guy comes over and asks if I am somebody. Then I don't know what I'll say.

# Michael Colleary

## Writing Partners

*"They might be the only writers in the history of television who were distraught when their show* wasn't *canceled."*

Michael Colleary is from a family of writers. His father is a television writer-producer. His brother is a television writer-producer. He's married to screenwriter and playwright Shannon Bradley. His brother-in-law is a screenwriter-director. Among his credits is *Face/Off* (written with Mike Werb), which *The New York Times* named among "The Best 1,000 Movies Ever Made."

My father's first job in television was holding cue cards for Clarabell the Clown in *The Howdy Doody Show*. It was the dawn of the industry, and nobody yet knew what television was or could be. My father didn't know how long the job on *Howdy Doody* would last or if a career was even possible.

Soon my dad was writing for *Captain Kangaroo* at CBS in Manhattan. *Kangaroo* became the Cadillac of kids' shows, airing five mornings a week and earning praise and Peabody Awards. My dad's success provided our family with a comfortable Ozzie-and-Harriet life in a leafy New Jersey suburb for almost 20 years.

When she wasn't chasing four kids, my mother was president of the PTA, a Den Mother in the Cub Scouts, and active in the local Women's Club. They were good, happy years, but when *Kangaroo* folded in the late 1970s, my parents learned just how tenuous a career in television can be.

My father looked around for work in New York City but found his options scant. Finally, my parents packed us up and moved us to Los Angeles so my dad could make a run at the sitcom business.

He was 47 years old.

My father didn't go to film school. He never wrote for *The Harvard Lampoon*. The number of people my parents knew when they landed in L.A. could be counted on one hand. None of them ran a network.

What my father had were powers of concentration honed by writing five one-hour television shows a week while on *Kangaroo*. And he had motivation. "Nothing will light a fire under your ass like having kids," he said. They had two in college and two in a Studio City girls' school.

But, most fortunately for my father, he had my mom. Although her name doesn't appear on any credit crawl, she was his partner. Her adamantine strength supported him and tended to us through all the stress, setbacks, financial uncertainty and murderously hard work that was to come.

That first year, my dad wrote his spec scripts in their bedroom. He had an electric typewriter on a typing stand and a stack of carbon paper. He sat there from 8 in the morning until lunch, ate a sandwich and drank a Diet Pepsi in the kitchen, then went back upstairs and worked until 6. I never saw him go out for coffee, flip through magazines, sun himself on the patio or pick up the phone.

He wrote and sipped Diet Pepsi and honed and smoked Carltons and polished. After dinner, my mother read his pages and gave him notes. Next morning, he was back at it. Next evening, so was my mother.

Opportunities started to appear, but somehow my parents knew they had to wait for the right one. "If you start off writing for bad shows," they told us, "that's where you'll stay." It must have been hard, turning away chances to work when they were almost broke. But they refused to risk my dad's shot by jumping on a dead-end show.

The first couple of years were full of uncertainty, but they never complained. They never believed that my father, pushing 50, couldn't break in, even though, at times, it must have seemed impossible.

My mother anchored our family life with birthdays, graduations and holidays. She was determined to provide us with the Eastern Christmases we all missed so much. Every year, she dragged home the biggest tree on the YMCA lot while admonishing, "Don't tell your father how much it cost!" At dinner, she agonized over the gravy while my father carved the bird. Our job was to smile when he marveled at our towering, lush, "20-dollar" Plantation Fir.

Finally my dad managed to get a meeting on a hit show. He arrived at the production office on time, then sat and waited while the two producers he was scheduled to see played chess in full view of him.

He sat there for half an hour. My parents had $300 left in the bank. They needed this job. But what was the job? Writing comedy? Or eating shit? So he left.

A lot of hope had been riding on that meeting. But my father knew my mother would approve. "You only have your name in this business," my mother would tell us. "If you don't respect yourself, no one else will."

To their credit, the producers chased after him. They apologized. They all went back inside and my father pitched his notions. They bought one. He wrote them a script. They put him on staff.

Every year, my parents did a little better. My dad's shows always scored solid if not spectacular ratings. That was okay with him. "Soon as you break the top ten, everybody thinks they're curing cancer." When your show is in the 30s, he explained, "everybody is just happy to have a job." And that was okay with my mom. She thought he was under enough pressure already.

Friday was taping day. My mother would drive my dad to the studio in the morning, then come back in the afternoon to sit with the audience. She'd stay until they finished in the late hours. Then she'd drive him back home.

Usually, he was pretty beat. My mother served him a lot of meals—where else?—in front of the television. She made sure he went to the doctor, saw friends, took naps, hit Swensen's with the kids. As the season ground on, the social engagements stopped. Food was medicine. Sleep was life-support. He'll tell you that he dreaded the weekends, dreaded hiatus, because starting up again was so much harder than just soldiering on.

But start over it did, every Monday. Week in, week out. The

first season of *Benson*, my father and one other writer were the whole staff. They wrote and produced 26 episodes. They might be the only writers in the history of television who were distraught when their show *wasn't* canceled.

And every Friday, my mom would be back in the audience. She always sat in the same place, where my dad could see her when he came down to the stage. When the show finally ended its run, they retired my mother's chair. Just pulled it up and gave it to her with a nice plaque. It's still in their family room.

I only saw my father discouraged once. One of the cast made a big show of dumping that week's script in the garbage. My dad didn't get angry. He said, "There isn't time to write them properly, there isn't time to rehearse them properly, there isn't time to direct them properly or edit them or score them. I am not the enemy. Time is the enemy." The classically trained actor stared at my father, then extracted the script from the trash. After that, he kept his critiques to himself.

"Time is the enemy." My father could handle the notes, the network, rewrite night, moody actors, gallons of diet soda and thousands of cigarettes, but he couldn't stop the years from passing, couldn't prevent the inevitable toll. One day, while working on the always chilly soundstage, he picked up a cold. Soon it erupted into double pneumonia.

By then my parents had spent a decade in the sitcom business. My dad had won an Emmy® for *Barney Miller*. He had helped lead *Benson* to the promised land of syndication. My mom made every dollar count, paying off their house and salting away their retirement, and still had something left over to spend on their grandchildren.

They had built a new life. It was time to live it.

They've been retired 15 years now. But I think they miss it.

Fifteen years later, my mom still watches every episode of my brother's show, whether he wrote it or not, and calls him afterwards.

Fifteen years later, my dad scours his local paper for stories worthy of the big screen and sends them to me.

Fifteen years later, writers I don't know still shake my hand when they find out I'm the son of Bridget and Bob Colleary.

And on Christmas day, my mother still agonizes over the gravy. My dad still carves the bird. Every year we have with them, my brother, sisters and I give grateful thanks.

They weren't trying to set an example. Maybe that's the best way.

The job is hard. The season is long. Applause fades. Cherish your dignity.

# Jeff Melvoin

## Saying Kaddish for Uncle Manny

*"As a feature film writer,
you toil in solitary misery.
As a TV writer, you work
in collective misery."*

Jeff Melvoin has worked in television as a writer-producer on *Remington Steele*, *Hill Street Blues*, *Northern Exposure*, *Picket Fences*, *Early Edition* and *Going to California* (enjoyed by dozens of Showtime viewers around the country). Awards include an Emmy®, two Golden Globes and a Television Critics Award. His family includes one wife, two sons and a wheaten terrier. His goal in life is to be home by six.

Writing on staff for a one-hour television series is a particularly rarified form of screenwriting. As a feature film writer, you toil in solitary misery. As a TV writer, you work in collective misery. You're surrounded by fellow writers. You break stories together, lunch together, gripe together, all under the guidance of an executive producer who is him or herself a writer.

An outsider might assume that this is a good thing for writers, to which you, the seasoned TV staffer would tartly reply, it depends. What you know about executive producers is that writing well and supervising others to write well are two distinct talents which don't necessarily come wrapped in the same mortal package.

Josh Brand, executive producer and co-creator of *Northern Exposure*, was the real deal. He could write and manage as well as anyone I'd encountered in Hollywood when I joined the staff in its first full season. What's more, unlike many executive producers, he did not want to write your script. He wanted *you* to write your script. But it didn't come easy (what good writing ever does?). Josh would give clinically precise, sometimes scathing notes, delivered with the calm and implacable assurance of a neurosurgeon dressing down an intern. If you could take it, great things could result. If you couldn't, you were gone—and quickly.

During my third season on the show, I had an idea that came out of left field one day. What would happen if (the watchword of any writer, "what would happen if") Dr. Joel Fleischman, our Jewish fish-out-of-water protagonist, needed a *minyan*? A *minyan* is a group of ten adult Jews required to perform certain rituals like regular Sabbath services. I thought it was funny. How the hell do you find nine other Jews in Cicely, Alaska? My next thought was, okay, why would Joel need a *minyan*? He's not going to get the sudden urge to hold a Sabbath service. I remembered that saying Kaddish, the prayer said for the dead, also required a *minyan*. I had an Uncle Bill I adored who was raised Orthodox in New York. What would happen if Joel's Uncle Manny died and his Aunt called from Florida to ask that Joel say Kaddish for him? Out of respect—and love—Joel would feel obligated. I began to get excited. This was a major "A" story (a typical episode involved an "A" story of some 12 to 14 "beats" or scenes, and two to three lesser stories, adding up to about 24 beats an episode). I had visions of the town pitching in to help, of various unlikely Jewish Alaskans being roped into Cicely, of a last-minute conclusion involving an open microphone to a scientific team member working on the polar cap, the tenth man of the *minyan*.

I threw together some notes and in the flush of discovery presented my pitch to Josh. "It's not an 'A' story," he said flatly. "Five to six beats max." I don't think I said, "You're wrong," but I did my best to convince him. No go. Fortunately, I had enough confidence in my relationship with Josh that I was able to say, okay, then, let's not do it. I had too much passion for the story to see it reduced to insignificance. I'd come up with something else for my next episode. Which I did. And for the next one after that.

But then came my next script and the well had gone pretty dry, so much so that I was reluctantly willing to offer up my Kaddish idea as a "B" story just to get something going. I went over my cut-down notes with Josh, who looked up at one point and said, "This is a bigger story. What would happen if the town tried to get a *minyan* for Joel?" And he proceeded to lay out essentially what I had pitched the first time around. Now I could have said, "That's what I suggested three months ago, remember?" Instead, like any staff member with a family to feed, I said, "That is a brilliant idea."

We rapidly proceeded to develop the story until we reached a point of major disagreement. In my original thinking, Joel eventually found his *minyan*. The story, in that sense, had a "happy" ending. Josh believed it was better if Joel not only didn't get his *minyan*, but actively decided against it. He thought it was less expected and made better drama. I could see his point, but as a Jew I found it troubling. Why would Joel reject a *minyan*? I struggled with it until a light dawned and I realized that I was not Joel Fleischman. It was a liberating thought. Could I find reasons for Joel to get uncomfortable with a *minyan*? Sure, and I wouldn't have to look very far, either.

For a long time, I had wondered whether organized religion hadn't done more throughout history to drive people apart than to bring them together. Here I had a chance to explore that theme. As the story laid out, once the town goes to bat for Joel, following a briefing by town heavyweight Maurice Minnifield on how to identify Jews (including a photo of Kirk Douglas as Spartacus), Joel begins to feel strange. His thoughts come to graphic climax in a dream sequence (we never had car chases or gunfights on *Northern Exposure*; when things got slow, we threw in a dream sequence). Joel imagines the main street of Cicely as the scene of a spaghetti western in which a posse of *"Minyan* rangers" rides in on horseback to get him. This outlandish scenario makes Joel reconsider the logic of searching high and low to find other Jews with whom he can honor his late uncle. In the final scene, held in the town church, Joel explains to the entire cast that the purpose of requiring a *minyan* to say Kaddish is to be sure that the mourner does not grieve alone but is among his community, a reminder both that his loss is shared by others and that life goes on. Joel has come to realize that the people sitting in these pews are his community. These are the people with whom he wants to share his grief. He proceeds to say Kaddish in Hebrew while others pray according to their individual customs and beliefs.

It was an ending that inspired as many Jewish viewers as it troubled. The episode became the subject of at least several sermons across the country that I know of because they were sent to me. The common complaint was that the script was a pretext for assimilation. I wrote back to politely disagree, but I wasn't going to change any minds. On the other hand, author Judith Krantz, a huge *Northern Exposure* fan, wrote me a lovely note to say that she thought the episode was a beautiful expression of Jewish thought. Go figure.

*Kaddish for Uncle Manny* was nominated for an Emmy® for "Outstanding Writing in a Drama Series." It lost to an episode of *Homicide: Life on the Streets* written by colleague Tom Fontana. But that's another story.

# Tom Fontana

## Broken Windows

---

*"I am proudest of a piece of writing which very few people saw and which no one in our business even noticed."*

After earning an Emmy® Award, two WGA Awards and three Peabody Awards for *Homicide: Life on the Street*, Tom Fontana created and Executive Produced *Oz*, which has won three CableACE Awards, including Best Drama, as well as the prize for Outstanding Series from The Cinema Tout Ecran Festival in France.

I had never written about the Holocaust. In fact, my knowledge of concentration camps was limited to, as a kid, seeing a documentary on the liberation of, if memory serves, Buchenwald and to my Catholic parents trying, fruitlessly, to explain the horror I was watching on my TV screen.

Flash forward to 1988: in New York, working with Bruce Paltrow and the Tinker brothers on our new series *Tattinger's*.

One night, I was at dinner with a couple my age, friends from Westchester, and the wife, a bright and articulate woman, began to talk about how her parents had survived Dachau and how, to her eternal frustration, they refused to speak of their lives back then. She described her guilt, growing up free and happy, complete with

Beatles and bubble gum, while her parents' youth, dark and terrifying, was totally unknown to her.

The next day, I mentioned all this to Noel Behn, the novelist, who had spent time exploring the camps in preparation for a book he'd written, *The Shadowboxer*. I asked Noel if he'd co-write an episode of *Tattinger's* with me about the children of the Holocaust. Noel agreed, but with a warning: "This way lies despair!!!"

We started doing intensive research: I read the books Noel assigned, we screened archival footage and went to a convention in New Jersey, where we met the sons and daughters of Holocaust survivors, each with their own unique and compelling story.

Over the many weeks that Noel and I worked on the script, something happened to me. Something that had never happened before—*I lost myself*.

In the one hundred or so hours of television I had written up to that point—stories dealing with abortion, testicular cancer, autism, homelessness, Salvadoran death squads, Ethiopian famine—I had never become so immersed in a subject, so utterly uninterested in my own day-to-day life. As I wrote and real life faded, I became sullen, testy, suspicious and afraid. The deeper I dug, I found more and more layers of evil. Pure and repulsive evil.

Ultimately, the evil turned on me and asked, not only "Would you let this happen?" but, far worse, "If some men are capable of such atrocities, aren't *all* men?" And, worst of all, "Are you?"

As we shot the episode (called *Broken Windows* with Uta Hagen and Maria Tucci in the guest leads), I began to emerge from the dank hole of isolation, the gloom dissipated and I could "do lunch" again.

Meanwhile, *Tattinger's* was on the brink of cancellation.

Brandon Tartikoff announced that we could only air ten of the eleven episodes we'd already filmed. Bruce left the decision up to me and so, instead of ending the series with a screwball comedy I'd co-written with John Tinker, called *Screwball*, I chose *Broken Windows* as our finale.

NBC had other ideas. The executives-in-charge wanted something light and funny. So, we did the honorable thing: we lied. We told the network that we couldn't possibly get *Screwball* out of post in time. Ironically, *Broken Windows* was the only episode of *Tattinger's* that went up in the ratings at the half hour.

I have been blessed in my career with long runs—*St. Elsewhere*, *Homicide: Life on the Street*, *Oz*—and have been given a slew of trophies, acknowledging whatever talent I have.

But I am proudest of a piece of writing which very few people saw and which no one in our business even noticed. Of course, maybe that's why I'm so proud.

Or maybe because instead of trying to transport the viewers, I was myself transported. I experienced the ultimate rush of being a writer—I was carried away by the truth.

# SECRETS OF THE HOLLYWOOD PROS #7:

## The Last Word

Our final secret to success in Hollywood comes in the form of our final essay. It's only appropriate that our last word should come from a writer who wrote some of television's first words, and some of the movies' and Broadway's funniest lines.

# Hal Kanter

## Don't Say it Again, Sam

---

*"For too many years, I was one of Samuel Johnson's blockheads."*

Hal Kanter, WGA's Paddy Chayefsky Laurel and Valentine Davies Awards winner, began reading at the age of three, writing at seven and has been doing both ever since, amassing credits from *Hellzapoppin'* on Broadway, *Bing Crosby* on radio, *Julia* on TV, *The Rose Tattoo*, seven Bob Hope features, Elvis Presley's *Loving You* and 26 other films, to one novel, one auto-biography and 30 Academy Awards® shows. He is currently weary.

Long ago, writers sold all rights to their scripts in perpetuity. To studios, "royalties" was a profanity. Residuals were unheard of.

Despite that, I sold a half-hour play to the Mutual Broadcasting System about a death-row prisoner who was given a chance to relive his life, for a motivation I can no longer defend.

It was a serious fantasy that was repeated several times on radio. All I recall is that my prisoner began a new life as an infant and wound up back on death row again.

That was a long time ago.

I was 18 years old.

A much longer time later, editor Daryl Nickens tantalized me with the challenge to relive my own life by writing about the things I would not do again but also burnishing a new life with things I would.

Can any author who has nothing on his mind more important than himself resist that opportunity?

**After several minutes of profound thought, here are some of the things I would *not* do again:**

Drive myself to finish a screenplay by Friday.

Drink while driving myself to finish it by Monday.

Hardly ever turn down a job.

Fight for a line unless I feel it's the last one I can write.

Believe even 10% of what any agent tells me or 90% that a producer promises.

Believe an exhibitor.

Trust a collaborator to show up by 10.

Take for granted that everything I write is great.

Try to beat Billy Wilder in the Word Game, even though he's dead.

Work with Norman Lear, Pinky Lee or Rex Harrison, even though some of them are dead.

Presume to tell witless wannabes how to write comedy.

Write dialogue in dialect lak dis hyeah.

Dismiss my wife's suggestions to improve what I consider perfection.

Hire a secretary who has no sense of humor, no matter what her bra size is.

Waste God's precious gift of time on a golf course when I could be fishing and reading.

Play Solitaire on my computer more than 20 minutes a day.

Spend thousands of dollars on tobacco that for 50 years I thought I had to smoke in order to write.

Forget to take a pencil and a stiff piece of paper to the bathroom when an idea hits me in the middle of the night.

Ever show a first draft to fools.

Send out for Chinese food to eat in the office at midnight.

Work seven days a week around the clock at any producer's whim.

When studios said I was too old to hire, add "II" to my byline on the next spec script.

Believe that my life's work is art, not business.

Collaborate with a writer who never wants to go home.

Use time making lists like this, when I could spend more of it with my children, eating sushi.

   That partial list of agonies is balanced by a shorter list of ecstasies.

Writing for radio, stage, screen, television, awards shows, public speeches and sarcasm to sports writers who are pretenders to humor have all provided me with more than the average share of pleasure, gratification, comfort, laughter and frequent haircuts.

**Given the chance to do it all again, the next time around, here are a few of the things I *would* do:**

Marry the same girl, who is still as beautiful as a second wife.

Finish college.

Finish high school.

Accept more offers to teach college courses.

Discover what I.A.L. stands for in Iz Diamond's name.

Stifle my compulsion to rewrite every script I produce before it goes to the table.

Write more of what I love, not what someone else likes.

Avoid working with anyone who takes three-hour lunches looking at new cars.

Realize how ignorant I was at the age of 17 instead of waiting to find out when I was 70.

Spend more time reading Mark Twain, Josh Billings and S.J. Perelman and less time trying to imitate them.

Many years ago, Samuel Johnson said, "No man but a blockhead ever wrote except for money." For too many years, I was one of Samuel Johnson's blockheads. If you want to write, are writing or trying to, just do it. Forget what the good Dr. Johnson said. It took me a lifetime to discover the importance of writing not for money alone, but with a passion that must be quenched, and the value of accepting criticism of that passion's product.

Honest criticism is frequently valid and should be respected, but praise is too often aftershave lotion: it should be sniffed, not swallowed.

P.S. Feel free to praise us for how much pleasure this book has given you.

# Afterword

## Credit Where Credit Is Due?:

### Finally!

Admit it: you looked up my credits on IMDb, the Internet Movie Database, to see who I am; and from that, have decided how seriously you should take what I say.

Which really pisses me off. It's not you; it's IMDb, which doesn't list four of the five major awards my work has won or for which it has been nominated. Their policy, apparently, is not to list anything that requires effort on their part to discern (such as certain major award nominations).

"What an egomaniac," you say. "Boo-fucking-hoo!"

Were that it was just a matter of ego. It's a matter of survival.

You are your credits.

Your credits are your "permanent record." They are the appearance people judge you by. What you did when you looked up my credits is what happens in the business 24/7.

That's one of the reasons why determining credits—who wrote

the movie or TV show—remains one of the most solemn duties and contentious issues Writers Guild members face.

Contentious because careers and fortunes ride on the outcome. Yet, for both film and television, the process of credit determination is the same: deceptively simple, yet maddeningly arcane. When a movie or TV show is finished, the company that made it makes a tentative credit determination and informs the writers who've worked on the project and the Guild of the result. If no one objects, that tentative credit becomes the final credit. But if one of the participating writers objects to those credits, a credit arbitration commences. (In film, if one of the participating writers is a "production executive," aka a director, studio executive or credited producer, an arbitration automatically ensues.)

In an arbitration, a three-writer panel, chosen by Guild staff from a list approved by the membership, separately reads all relevant drafts, and by applying the rules contained in the Guild's Credit Manual, comes to a credit determination. Guild staff also appoint a Consultant, a member who has had experience in credit arbitrations, to guide the process. The Consultant doesn't guide by reading the material; if asked for help by any of the Arbiters (which usually happens when none of the three agree), the Consultant attempts to create consensus by asking Socratic questions. Arbiter: "What constitutes 50% of a script?" Consultant: "What do you think constitutes 50% of this script?" When two of three arbiters offer the same credits, the arbitration concludes. Unless someone objects. In which case, there is an appeals process.

While the Guild's formulas for assigning credit are specific and seemingly objective, the application of the criteria, as well as their definition, is deeply subjective. Seldom is the outcome of a credit determination obvious from the start. The only thing that's certain is someone is going to be extremely upset at the outcome, which is why there was an arbitration in the first place.

The stakes are high. Writing a successful high-profile project confers a place on the "A" list (at least for awhile). For the duration of your membership in that exclusive club, every other project remotely in the genre of your hit is pitched to you. And while you're determining what hook to bite, if any, you are sustained by the money you made on your success, most of which typically comes in the form of a production bonus, which is payable on the start of principal photography to the credited writers. (Usually, the amount for sole credit is double the amount of shared credit.) And, of course, when the project reruns on cable, DVD, airlines, free TV, both domestic and foreign, and "any and all media, known and unknown, throughout the universe" (as the Certificate of Authorship in your contract stipulates), residuals go to the credited writers in proportion to their credit.

Is anyone surprised, then, that credit arbitrations often end up as a legal showdown: lawyers at ten paces?

Thankfully, that won't be happening here.

There will be no whispering about who really wrote the essays in this book. Each is the sole responsiblity of the credited writers. For which, each has my undying gratitude. I hope they have deepened your understanding of what it's like to write for the Hollywood screen as much as they have deepened mine.

# ALPHABETICAL INDEX OF CONTRIBUTORS

## ESSAYS

# SECRETS OF THE HOLLYWOOD PROS

# The Writers Guild
# Foundation

The Writers Guild Foundation was established in 1966 as a non-profit charitable corporation by a group of television and motion picture writers, members of the Writers Guild of America, west. The founding president was James. R. Webb. The Foundation's mission is to preserve and promote excellence in writing and to advance the recognition of the writer's unique contribution to the art of film and television.

The Foundation's major programs are:

- **The Writers Guild Foundation Shavelson-Webb Library**, housing over 15,000 film and television scripts and a reference collection of books, tapes and photographs related to writers and writing and to the history of writers in Hollywood;

- An ongoing program of educational seminars, panel discussions, screenings and other writer events, including **Writers on Writing, Writers on Genre, Spring Storytellers** and regular summer craft events;

- An **academic outreach** program with schools and colleges, including a Visiting Writer Program and videoconferencing services available to film schools, colleges and universities nationwide;

- Literacy and young people's programs in Los Angeles, including an annual book drive, school-based writing camps for at-risk teens, a mentor referral service for K-12 school programs and school/classroom visits as requested;

- Conferences and international exchanges, including **Words into Pictures**, a major forum for film and television writers;

- **Oral history** interviews, including *The Writer Speaks*, a series of video interviews with the great writers of classic film and television, plus interviews with Writers Guild members about Writers Guild and labor history in Hollywood;

- *Words*, a short film highlighting and celebrating the writer's contribution to some of the great moments in motion pictures;

- *Publishing* partnerships, including the books *The First Time I Got Paid for It, Ten Minutes to the Pitch, Doing It For Money* and other titles.

The Foundation is a 501 ( c ) 3 non-profit corporation. Its activities are funded by voluntary contributions from writers and industry friends. Most of its programs and events are open to the public. For further information contact:

**The Writers Guild Foundation**
7000 West Third Street, Los Angeles, CA 90048-4329
Telephone (323) 782-4692   Fax (323) 782-4695

Published by

Los Angeles